Sustainable Project-Based Learning

Five Steps for Designing Authentic Classroom Experiences in Grades 5–12

Brad Sever

Foreword by Suzie Boss

Solution Tree | Press

a division of
Solution Tree

555 North Morton Street
Bloomington, IN 47404
800.733.6786 (toll free) / 812.336.7700
FAX: 812.336.7790

email: info@SolutionTree.com
SolutionTree.com

Visit **go.SolutionTree.com/21stcenturyskills** to download the free reproducibles in this book.

Printed in the United States of America

Library of Congress Cataloging-in-Publication Data

Names: Sever, Brad, author.

Title: Sustainable project-based learning : five steps for designing
    authentic classroom experiences in grades 5-12 / Brad Sever.

Description: Bloomington : Solution Tree Press, [2022] | Includes
    bibliographical references and index.

Identifiers: LCCN 2021060995 (print) | LCCN 2021060996 (ebook) | ISBN
    9781952812330 (paperback) | ISBN 9781952812347 (ebook)

Subjects: LCSH: Project method in teaching. | Social learning. | Emotional
    intelligence.

Classification: LCC LB1027.43 .S48 2022 (print) | LCC LB1027.43 (ebook) |
    DDC 371.3/6--dc23

LC record available at https://lccn.loc.gov/2021060995

LC ebook record available at https://lccn.loc.gov/2021060996

Solution Tree
Jeffrey C. Jones, CEO
Edmund M. Ackerman, President

Solution Tree Press
President and Publisher: Douglas M. Rife
Associate Publisher: Sarah Payne-Mills
Managing Production Editor: Kendra Slayton
Editorial Director: Todd Brakke
Art Director: Rian Anderson
Copy Chief: Jessi Finn
Senior Production Editor: Christine Hood
Content Development Specialist: Amy Rubenstein
Acquisitions Editor: Sarah Jubar
Copy Editor: Jessi Finn
Proofreader: Mark Hain
Text Designer: Fabiana Cochran
Cover Designer: Laura Cox
Editorial Assistants: Charlotte Jones, Sarah Ludwig, and Elijah Oates

To Brock and Ella,

On the road to accomplishing your dreams, you will face challenges.
May you always have the courage and strength to persevere through those challenges.

Love always and unconditionally,

Dad

ACKNOWLEDGMENTS

There are so many people I would like to thank. First, I want to thank my beautiful wife, Rachel, for her love and honesty throughout this entire process. Thank you for allowing me to pursue this work that I love so much. I appreciate the sacrifices you have had to make on my behalf. You inspire me to be a better parent and a better educator. I am so fortunate to be your husband.

Brock and Ella, thank you for all your affirmation throughout my time working on this project. From the beginning, you knew this was a goal I had, and your kind words motivated me to keep working. I am extremely lucky to be your dad.

I would like to thank my parents, David and Cheryl Sever. From the time I was very young, I knew I wanted to be an educator just like both of you. Growing up, you modeled for me what it should look like to maintain a family-and-work balance. Thank you for your love and encouragement.

To my brother Michael—thanks for being the best big brother a guy could have. I appreciate your praise for this work.

Ally, thank you for being an amazing teacher. I am inspired by your humble and consistent service to others.

To Genna, J.D., and Addy—you inspire me with your work ethic. Each of you has your own interests and passions, and you not only work hard, but you always treat people with kindness.

Don and Ann, thank you for your love and support.

Professionally, there are several people for whom I am eternally grateful. If not for them, this book would not have been published.

Michael McDowell, your work and friendship have had a significant influence on this project. Thank you for challenging my thinking and for devoting your professional life to making learning experiences more meaningful for kids.

Suzie Boss, you wrote the first project-based learning book I ever read, and your support and belief in me are why I was able to start this project with Solution Tree. Words truly cannot express my gratitude for you.

Claudia Wheatley, thank you for believing in me, for your honesty, and for your mentorship.

Amy Rubenstein, you gave my ideas a clear voice. Thank you for your extremely helpful expertise.

Christine Hood, thank you for the time and effort you put into the constructive feedback you provided.

To my amazing friends and colleagues Brian Schoch, Aaron Eisberg, Matt Baer, and Eric White—thank you for your insight, humor, and kindness. I value all of our conversations. I am fortunate to collaborate with each of you.

John Larmer, thank you for the body of work you have written on project-based learning. You are a project-based learning pioneer, and I so appreciate you.

Shayla Adams, thank you for your friendship, wisdom, and insight.

Thank you to the teachers who contributed to this book, including my lifelong friend Craig Harper. Craig, you are an outstanding educator.

Thank you to Cristen Cassler, Kara House, Dan Perdun, Paul Crofts, Christopher Kjaer, Joel Haynie, Stephanie Barnes, and Amanda Clark. I am so grateful to have worked with each of you.

Thank you to Gavin Hays, Jeff Phillips, Kim Taylor, and Tom O'Toole for your leadership in this work.

Kyle Miller, thank you for being such a man of integrity as well as for your commitment to and vision for mental health.

Joe Belser, thank you for your lifelong friendship and your consistent words of kindness, encouragement, and humor.

Thanks to Steve Loser, Matt Clodfelter, Doug Sisk, Shannon Singleton, Carey Munoz, Tina Waechter, Sandi Squire, and Joy Seybold. My experience with all of you at Ben Davis High School so many years ago planted the seed that grew into this work. I savor the memories of us working together.

Thank you to the instructional coaches at Carmel High School both past and present. I am grateful to have had the opportunity to work with each of you.

Finally, thank you to all the educators I have worked with around the United States and in Australia. You have all made me better.

Solution Tree Press would like to thank the following reviewers:

Pamela Bourgeois
Principal, Kleb Intermediate School, Instructional
    Officer for Professional Learning (Retired)
Klein Independent School District
Klein, Texas

Lori Jeschke
Director of Education
Prairie Spirit School Division
Warman, Saskatchewan

Jed Kees
Principal
Onalaska Middle School
Onalaska, Wisconsin

Mike Pickles
Educator, Author, Consultant, and Podcaster
Yellowknife, Northwest Territories

Jennifer Steele
Assistant Principal
Northside High School
Fort Smith, Arkansas

Natalie Vardabasso
Assessment Instructional Design Lead
Calgary Academy
Calgary, Alberta

Visit **go.SolutionTree.com/21stcenturyskills** to
download the free reproducibles in this book.

TABLE OF CONTENTS

ABOUT THE AUTHOR

Brad Sever serves as an assistant principal at Carmel High School in Carmel, Indiana. During his time in this position, he helped create and sustain a successful instructional-coaching program and grow the school's International Baccalaureate program, as well as parts of the dual-credit program. Brad also served as the school testing coordinator and 504 coordinator, and oversaw the social studies, mathematics, and science departments.

Brad has been an educator since 2002. Prior to his current role, Brad served as a project-based learning (PBL) coach and an instructional coach in a large urban district, an assistant principal for an expeditionary learning charter school, and a teacher at a middle school where he helped develop an integrated social studies and language arts PBL course.

Brad is a national presenter, speaking on project-based learning, instructional coaching, and leadership. He has consulted for over one hundred schools around the United States and Australia. He has provided professional development for charter schools and urban, rural, and suburban schools. Since 2010, he has served as a national faculty member for PBLWorks (formerly the Buck Institute for Education).

Brad holds a bachelor of science in secondary social studies education from Huntington University and a master of arts in educational leadership from Ball State University. He has over thirty hours of coursework completed toward his EdS in educational leadership, also from Ball State University. Brad is trained in cognitive coaching, expeditionary learning, and the International Baccalaureate Diploma Programme, and he has attended numerous trainings on equity and inclusion. His practical approach to professional development comes from the variety of experiences and perspectives he has gained.

To learn more about Brad's work, visit the Sustainable Project-Based Learning website (www.perseveranceeducation.com), or follow him @BradSever on Twitter.

To book Brad Sever for professional development, contact pd@SolutionTree.com.

FOREWORD

By Suzie Boss

In their quest to better prepare students for the challenges and opportunities ahead, schools are turning to project-based learning (PBL) as the answer. As a longtime advocate of PBL, I'm encouraged by this momentum. High-quality PBL can deliver a wide range of benefits, from increased student engagement and deeper learning to development of nonacademic competencies that are essential for college, careers, and active citizenship.

But the truth is PBL also raises a host of questions. Educators who are new to this approach ask about everything from curriculum ("How will I ever cover the content?") to teaching strategies ("What's the teacher's role in student-centered learning?") to assessment ("How will we evaluate students' work if they all make different products?") to initiative overload ("How will we ever find time for this?").

Brad Sever doesn't shy away from the hard questions. Instead, he leverages them to guide readers through their own deep inquiry experiences. His background as a veteran PBL teacher, school leader, and instructional coach makes him an ideal guide for the journey. His classroom-tested tools and research-based strategies will help readers reach their ultimate destination: better outcomes for students.

What's unique about Sever's model is its emphasis on *sustainable* PBL (SPBL) as a comprehensive framework for instruction. Too many teachers have seen PBL rollouts start strong but lose steam as other worthy initiatives compete for attention, resources, and time for professional learning. That can lead to frustration, with teachers losing energy for making the shift to student-centered learning. SPBL works best—for students and teachers alike—when school systems align it with their overall vision for student success.

Increasingly, schools are engaging with their communities to clarify what students should know and be able to do by the time they graduate. Schools typically summarize the resulting vision statements with a portrait of a graduate that appears on posters, websites, and classroom walls.

But coming up with an appealing graphic is just the start. To realize their new visions, school systems must tackle the hard work of aligning instruction, assessment, and professional learning with their North Star.

Sever offers a valuable framework to help educators navigate this backward-design challenge. His approach is not to start from scratch when it comes to teaching and learning. Instead, he integrates well-established practices: academically rigorous PBL, social and emotional learning (SEL), collaborative teamwork, and high-impact instructional strategies. In his framework, these are not one-off or optional initiatives; they are all essential to making PBL sustainable. As he reminds us throughout this book, the destination is not fidelity to a particular PBL model but rather increased student learning. SPBL provides the means to get there.

Readers who start from different levels of familiarity with PBL will find plenty to think about in the chapters ahead. Newcomers will find clear definitions to build their PBL vocabulary and tools to scaffold project planning. Those with more PBL experience will be challenged to consider SEL goals for their projects alongside academic outcomes at the surface, deep, and transfer levels of learning.

In SPBL, teachers are not only intentional designers of student learning; they are also learners themselves. Sever's framework emphasizes action research as core to the work of being a PBL teacher. By collaborating to investigate problems of practice, teachers can overcome PBL pitfalls and fine-tune projects to meet the needs of diverse learners. When teachers examine student work together, they clarify what it means to see evidence of student growth in PBL. They can brainstorm formative strategies to keep learning on track. When they set goals for improvement, they challenge each other to pursue more equitable outcomes for all students. School leaders and instructional coaches can support teachers in this important work by providing them with time and tools to build their collective efficacy.

Although Sever advocates using collaborative teams as a core component of SPBL, he acknowledges that not every school dedicates time for teacher collaboration. He offers advice for teachers who are on solo journeys to help them build their own efficacy with sustainable PBL.

This thought-provoking book arrives at a critical time for education as schools continue to wrestle with student learning loss, disengagement, and teacher burnout resulting from the COVID-19 pandemic. How can you design a new normal for teaching and learning that prepares all students for the challenges ahead? Anyone who has spent time in a PBL environment will recognize that as a compelling driving question. With this book, Brad Sever provides you with a road map to help you discover your own solutions.

INTRODUCTION

Project-based learning (PBL) has intrigued me for more than sixteen years. Maybe it is because as a student, I loved understanding real-world applications of what I was learning. It could be because as a teacher, instructional coach, administrator, and consultant, I have seen PBL empower students from all grade levels, contexts, subjects, and demographics. I not only have seen what it has done for students, but also for teachers. I have seen teachers who were on the verge of retirement discover PBL and become reinvigorated. Throughout this book, I describe what it's like to have a relationship with PBL. So, whether you are new to your relationship with PBL or you have had a long relationship with it, there is something in this book for you. I come to this work as a practitioner and also as a student.

Let's begin this journey with the hypothetical case study of Nishtiv School District—perhaps you can relate to it.

Case Study: Nishtiv School District

Nishtiv School District (NSD) is a large public school district on the East Coast of the United States. The district consists of twelve elementary schools, three middle schools, and one large comprehensive high school. Nishtiv has a graduation rate of 73 percent. The graduation rate over the last five years has fluctuated between 71 percent and 76 percent. Within that five-year time frame, NSD has either formed a committee for or implemented each of the following initiatives.

- Social and emotional learning

- Grading practices

- Diversity, equity, and inclusion

- Professional learning community coalition

- Response to intervention

continued ▶

- Understanding by design
- Visible learning practices (Visible Learning+, n.d.), based on John A. C. Hattie's (2009) research
- Differentiated instruction
- Real-world learning for college and careers

NSD has worked hard to write and receive multiple professional development grants so teachers have been able to receive text resources and, on several occasions, attend trainings and seminars on some of these topics.

NSD administration displays a deep passion for providing teachers with professional development and professional learning opportunities. The administrators are willing to do whatever it takes to grow the plateauing graduation rate. However, the results of a recent school culture survey that NSD administered to all the teachers on campus raised some eyebrows. The survey was anonymous, and the teachers responded honestly. Seventy-two percent of teachers stated that they feel "overwhelmed," 31 percent stated that they "are considering looking for jobs at other schools," and 84 percent stated that they are "unclear of the school's mission and vision."

In addition to not reaching its graduation rate goals, NSD has another problem. The staff are suffering from initiative fatigue. Certainly, professional development is important, and all the initiatives have some level of value, but the district also should consider the well-being of the staff. As the staff survey indicated, this is a glaring issue. Instead of looking at each of these initiatives separately, NSD would benefit from a comprehensive instructional framework that incorporates elements of all the previously listed initiatives. Perhaps NSD would benefit from providing structures and procedures to discuss the following three questions.

1. How do you ensure at least one year's growth in one year's time?

2. How do you ensure an equal intensity of surface-, deep-, and transfer-level learning for each unit of study?

3. How do you define and provide intentional feedback to students on their growth in both content knowledge and SEL skills?

NSD would benefit from a comprehensive framework that incorporates not only research-based practices for unit planning but also clear and practical steps for conducting action research on its effectiveness. Ultimately, the district should implement the elements and steps of sustainable project-based learning (SPBL).

Although the preceding case study is a hypothetical example, if you can relate to challenges with too many initiatives, the process and templates in this book will be helpful.

Over the course of twenty years in education, I have had the privilege of serving as a PBL teacher and instructional coach, an administrator who helps facilitate PBL professional development, and a consultant for PBL through several different organizations, running workshops across the United States. As much as I love PBL, when I talk with teachers and other administrators who have implemented it, they have the same questions about teacher collaboration time and PBL.

- "How do we use teacher collaboration time more efficiently and effectively so we focus on the evidence of learning?"

- "How might we use discussion tools, such as protocols, during teacher collaboration time so all teachers feel confident in contributing to conversations in which they not only analyze student standardized test data but also the quality of student work?"

- "How should we best structure and discuss our formative assessments?"

- "PBL takes too long to plan and implement. How is it sustainable?"

- "How do we ensure that students are learning the content and social and emotional skills at deep and transfer levels?"

Also, as both an educator and a parent, I have deeply reflected on the significance of social and emotional learning (SEL). Addressing issues of self-awareness, responsible decision making, and social awareness are things both students and adults can benefit from. As I talk with school counselors, teachers, and administrators across the United States regarding SEL, their questions include the following.

- "How should we define and assess SEL?"

- "How might SEL be genuinely integrated into the curriculum and not siloed or set aside as a separate initiative?"

- "How do we place a high value on SEL while still maintaining a focus on our core content?"

This book is different from other PBL books because it describes how to practically integrate SEL and teacher action research into the PBL process, in addition to emphasizing a focus on evidence of student learning as opposed to fidelity of implementation to the pedagogy. These are the aspects that make PBL more sustainable than typical PBL models.

The Purpose of This Book

This book provides a clear road map to plan, implement, and sustain a PBL unit grounded in research-based practices and focused on evidence of student learning in both content and SEL skills.

It emphasizes PBL *sustainability*, addressing the challenges of the pedagogy and clearly explaining how to identify and assess SEL skills for each unit. This ensures that the "juice is worth the squeeze" because students are not only growing in content knowledge but also in SEL skills. In addition, this book goes beyond reflection on PBL elements and dives deep into conducting action research around the evidence of student learning produced throughout each unit of study.

How is *sustainable* project-based learning (SPBL) different from just project-based learning (PBL)? First, it is a more comprehensive instructional framework. If SPBL were a vacation, it would be at an all-inclusive resort. Just like an all-inclusive resort, this book provides everything you need to plan, implement, and sustain high-quality teaching and learning.

The audience for this book is grades 5–12 educators, instructional coaches, and administrators who are interested in learning about a research-based, comprehensive instructional framework. Although this process can be done successfully with an individual teacher, this book is best used as part of a book study with teams of educators, such as teacher teams, administrative teams, curriculum teams, or any other collaborative team structure with members who have a passion for providing meaningful and authentic learning experiences for students. Part of the *sustainable* PBL process is teacher action research. Working in teams allows for deeper inspection and conversations around evidence of student learning.

What's in This Book

This book is organized into two parts. Part I, The *What* and *Why* of Project-Based Learning, contains four chapters. Chapter 1 explains why PBL can be a valuable methodology to promote meaningful learning experiences for students. Chapter 2 focuses on the seven design elements of SPBL and some of SPBL's challenges and even weaknesses. Chapter 3 offers strategies for maintaining a sustainable relationship with PBL, and chapter 4 explains why and how SEL should be integrated into the curriculum.

Part II, The *How* of Sustainable Project-Based Learning, is the heart of the book. Over five chapters, it outlines the five-step process for how to plan and implement PBL so it is truly sustainable. Chapter 5 covers step 1, planning the SPBL unit, which includes the following five stages: (1) create a learning intention (major concepts) for both academic content and SEL; (2) develop content and SEL success criteria for each level of learning (surface, deep, and transfer); (3) craft the driving question at the transfer level, adding authentic context for the unit; (4) create tasks that align with the success criteria; and (5) create an entry event to launch the sustained-inquiry process. Chapter 6 covers step 2, developing sustainable PBL assessments, which includes generating a performance rubric that includes clear evidence of learning, creating written pre- and postassessments to measure quantitative growth, and creating anticipated student-generated questions based on the driving question or challenge they are trying to solve. In SPBL, we call these *need-to-knows*. Chapter 7 covers step 3, establishing a clear goal for student learning. Chapter 8 covers step 4, conducting teacher action research, and chapter 9 covers step 5, reflecting, refining, and celebrating the successful completion of an authentic learning process. Finally, chapter 10 summarizes the process while also emphasizing that we, as educators, should not only ask key questions about evidence of student learning but also about our own personal and professional growth through self-reflection.

Each chapter ends with a summary and questions for reflection, as well as a challenge to reinforce information from the chapter and promote next steps. You could use these questions for a collaborative book study or simply for individual reflection. In addition, some chapters feature perspectives from the field, which are written by teachers and administrators who have unique experiences in this work. You will find templates, charts, and practical tools to help you plan and implement a unit of study that incorporates core content, social and emotional learning, and teacher action research. Included are tips on raising awareness about equity and inclusion and clear definitions of common educational buzzwords.

The book concludes with three helpful appendices. Appendix A is a glossary of key terms used throughout the book. Appendix B offers a protocol library that includes helpful protocols for teachers to use both in the classroom and during teacher collaboration time. Appendix C contains examples of teacher-completed SPBL units across various content areas and grade levels. These appendices provide tools to support conversation and implementation of the work.

Summary

This book is different than other PBL books. Not only does it define PBL, it also addresses its weaknesses and applies practice tools and research. You will walk away with clear steps to plan an SPBL unit that integrates and assesses SEL, and promotes teacher action research centered around evaluating evidence of student learning. Within these pages, you will find a comprehensive instructional framework that promotes research-based, rigorous, and authentic learning experiences for students that they can apply outside school walls now and in the future.

PART I

THE *WHAT* AND *WHY* OF PROJECT-BASED LEARNING

CHAPTER 1

DEFINING SUSTAINABLE
PROJECT-BASED LEARNING

In the classic movie *The Karate Kid* (Weintraub & Avildsen, 1984), high school student Daniel LaRusso moves from New Jersey to California with his mother. Quickly, Daniel befriends maintenance man and karate expert Mr. Miyagi, who agrees to train Daniel after Daniel comes across a gang of bullies from the Cobra Kai dojo. But instead of providing standard training, Miyagi gives Daniel a series of rigorous chores to do around his house. Miyagi makes Daniel sand his deck, paint his fence, wax his cars, and paint his house. In a famous scene, Daniel gets angry with Miyagi and says, "I am being your slave." Miyagi responds by stating, "Daniel-san, come here. Show me sand the floor. . . . Now show me wax on, wax off. . . . Show me paint the fence" (Weintraub & Avildsen, 1984). To Daniel's surprise, he is able to block Miyagi's hits by simulating the motions from each of these chores.

Miyagi is a great teacher, not only because he develops a positive rapport with Daniel and maintains high expectations, but also because he understands the concept of teaching for transfer. Miyagi realizes that by having Daniel complete chores, Daniel will be able to apply what he learns from these tasks to a new and different context. Isn't that what we want as teachers? We want students to be able to apply the content and skills they learn in our classrooms to new and different situations and contexts, perhaps when taking a standardized test or faced with a challenging scenario several years after graduation.

Just like Mr. Miyagi, we have the option to use teaching methods in which we challenge students to apply their content knowledge and skills in new and authentic contexts. PBL is an excellent instructional framework to teach for transfer and allow students to showcase their content knowledge and skills in an authentic context. By incorporating clearly defined skills and conducting teacher action research rooted in conversations around evidence of student learning, it can be sustained.

A Definition of Project-Based Learning

PBLWorks (www.pblworks.org; formerly the Buck Institute for Education) has been around since 1987. I have had the privilege of working as a member of the National Faculty for PBLWorks since 2010. For the vast majority of its existence, PBLWorks has primarily focused on leading and refining professional development on project-based learning. PBLWorks (n.d.) defines *project-based learning* as "a teaching method in which students gain knowledge and skills by working for an extended period to investigate and respond to an authentic, engaging, and complex question, problem, or challenge." Along with that definition, PBLWorks (2021) states that PBL units should consist of seven design elements:

1. **A challenging problem or question:** The project is framed by a meaningful problem to be solved or a question to answer, at the appropriate level of challenge.

2. **Sustained inquiry:** Students engage in a rigorous, extended process of posing questions, finding resources, and applying information.

3. **Authenticity:** The project involves real-world contexts, tasks and tools, quality standards, or impact, or the project speaks to personal concerns, interests, and issues in the students' lives.

4. **Student voice and choice:** Students make some decisions about the project, including how they work and what they create, and express their ideas in their own voice.

5. **Reflection:** Students and teachers reflect on the learning, the effectiveness of their inquiry and [unit] activities, the quality of student work, and obstacles that arise and strategies for overcoming them.

6. **Critique and revision:** Students give, receive, and apply feedback to improve their process and products.

7. **Culminating public product:** Students make their [unit] work public by sharing it with and explaining or presenting it to people beyond the classroom.

Teachers designing true project-based learning units must make a conscious effort to incorporate all seven design elements into their units of study. The number of content standards learned should determine the duration of the unit. The more standards or the larger the concept, the longer the unit length that is justified. Teachers should make a conscious effort to incorporate all seven elements into their PBL units, although the level of each element for individual units may vary depending on the content, the students' readiness level, or the teacher's comfort with managing the process. For example, a teacher implementing PBL for the first time may incorporate voice and choice but not have the comfort level to incorporate it quite as deeply as a veteran PBL teacher. I elaborate on the idea of adjusting the levels of each element in chapter 2 (page 21).

Figure 1.1 shows the seven essential design elements of PBL. Intentionally incorporating all seven PBL design elements within a unit design is considered gold-standard PBL by PBLWorks (n.d.).

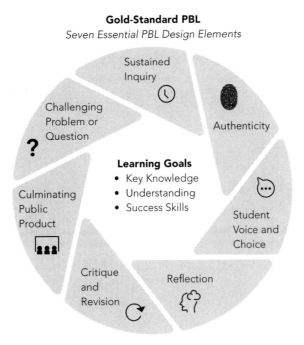

Source: PBLWorks, n.d. Used with permission.

Figure 1.1: Gold-standard PBL.

While figure 1.1 establishes the essential design elements of PBL, figure 1.2 provides a visual for what the process might look like when those design elements are implemented in a unit, from start to finish. Figure 1.2 and figure 1.3 (page 12) illustrate the difference between engaging in PBL and simply doing a project.

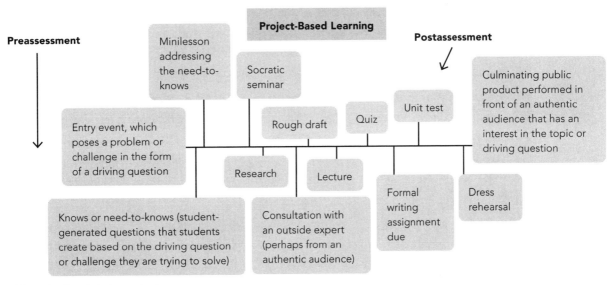

- The unit of study is the project.
- The teacher is expert in process as well as content.
- The teacher plans anticipated minilessons or lectures but also provides time for minilessons based on student-generated need-to-knows.
- Need-to-knows are used as a daily formative assessment, and the teacher stays true to the inquiry process.
- Minimal front-loading occurs.

Figure 1.2: Project-based learning.

When the seven design elements are implemented within the context of a unit of study, the unit might follow a sequence that looks similar to figure 1.2 (page 11). The unit starts with a driving question to ignite the sustained-inquiry process. Through an intentional sequence of formative assessments, feedback, and tasks, students engage in this systematic process. The project is the learning. The product produced provides clear evidence of student learning.

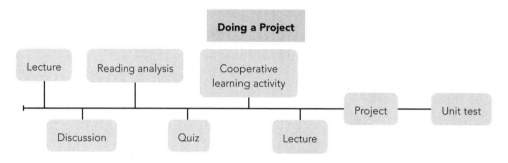

Figure 1.3: Doing a project.

Doing a project is not bad instruction. Students can certainly have a valuable learning experience doing a project. However, it is important to distinguish that implementing a PBL unit, including all the design elements, is much different and more effective than simply having students do a project.

Research Supporting PBL

In 2021, Lucas Education Research released two major studies of more than 6,000 students in 114 different schools across the United States (Krajcik et al., 2021; Saavedra et al., 2021). More than 50 percent of the students involved in the studies were from low-income households.

The research found that "of 3,645 students in five school districts, students in project-based learning AP classes outperformed those in traditional AP classes, improving test pass rates by 8 percentage points" (Saavedra et al., 2021, as cited in Terada, 2021). Thirty-seven percent of students in traditional Advanced Placement (AP) government and environmental science classrooms passed the AP exam compared to 45 percent of students who came from PBL classrooms (Saavedra et al., 2021).

The research concludes that not only do high school students in a PBL classroom outperform those in a traditional classroom on the AP exam, but elementary-aged students benefit from PBL as well (Krajcik et al., 2021; Saavedra et al., 2021). In the study, the researchers tracked data of 2,371 third-grade students. PBL raised the average science test scores. The data also showed that students at all reading levels "outperformed their counterparts in traditional classrooms" (Krajcik et al., 2021; Saavedra et al., 2021). If this research is not enough to convince educators of PBL's effectiveness (considering it is proven to enhance learning for elementary school– and high school–aged students in low-income areas), there is one more point to make. The research conducted in the AP government and AP environmental science classrooms concludes, "When teachers in the study taught the same curriculum for a second year, PBL students outperformed students in traditional classrooms by 10 percentage points [up from 8 the previous year]" (Terada, 2021). This means that not only was the PBL methodology more effective than traditional teaching, but after the second year of PBL curriculum implementation, when teachers' collective efficacy had increased, the level of learning grew even more.

Other educational research important to consider is the work of education researcher and author John Hattie. As of 2021, Hattie has accumulated more than twenty-five years of educational research connected to "more than 1,700 meta-analyses comprising more than 100,000 studies involving 300 million students around the world" (Visible Learning, n.d.). The scale that Hattie used to determine the effectiveness of the more than eight hundred meta-analyses was *effect size*. The formula for effect size is: effect size equals the mean of the experimental group minus the mean of the control group (standard deviation). In other words, this is the formula Hattie uses to create a scale to measure the effectiveness of each influence. He examines a variety of influences, including teaching practices, curricula, teacher, school, home, and student. The average effect size for Hattie's research is 0.4, meaning any influence researched that earned an effect size of 0.4 or higher is said to have more than one year's growth in one year (Visible Learning, n.d.). Visible Learning (n.d.), which works in collaboration with John Hattie, defines PBL as follows:

> In problem-based learning scenarios, students often act in groups and decide what they need to learn to resolve a particular problem or question, while teachers act as facilitators. It usually involves real-world problems to promote student learning of concepts and principles as opposed to direct presentation of facts and concepts. The aim is also to promote critical thinking skills, problem-solving abilities, and communication skills.

Critics of PBL argue that one of the most comprehensive educational research studies rated problem-based learning as earning an effect size of 0.35 (Visible Learning Meta[X], n.d.). As of November 2021, according to Corwin's Visible Learning Meta[X] (2021), Hattie used nine hundred studies and twenty-three meta-analyses to determine this effect size. This is slightly different from what Hattie determined in 2009, when he rated problem-based learning with a 0.15 effect size using 285 studies and eight meta-analyses (Hattie, 2009, p. 211).

Advocates for PBL should take a close look at this research. They should view it in two different ways. First, they should recognize that PBL is a comprehensive instructional framework, not a strategy. Second, they should realize that some of the influences that have the highest effect sizes from Hattie's research should be incorporated within the context of a PBL unit. For example, direct instruction and classroom discussions are strategies; they are not comprehensive instructional frameworks. Teachers should integrate direct instruction and classroom discussions within the context of a PBL unit. Figure 1.4 (page 14) displays several strategies Hattie identifies as having high impact on learning. In chapter 5 (page 69), you will explore how you can intentionally integrate these strategies into the specific tasks crafted for each success criterion in the PBL unit.

Influence	Effect Size
Self-reported grades	1.33
Jigsaw method	1.20
Response to intervention	1.09
Success criteria	0.88
Micro-teaching	0.88
Transfer strategies	0.86
Teacher clarity	0.84
Classroom discussion	0.82
Self-judgment and reflection	0.75
Reciprocal teaching	0.74
Summarization	0.74
Problem-solving teaching	0.67
Feedback	0.64
Metacognition strategies	0.60
Direct instruction	0.59
Appropriately challenging goals	0.59
Creativity programs	0.58
Inquiry-based teaching	0.46
Problem-based learning	0.35

Source: Visible Learning Meta^X, n.d.

Figure 1.4: High-impact strategies from Hattie's research.

Based on Hattie's research, PBL has a relatively low impact on learning, less than one year's growth in one year's time. So, if one of the most comprehensive educational research studies tells us that there are other methods that promote student learning more than PBL . . . *why* PBL?

The *Why* of PBL

Three key factors support the *why* of PBL.

1. PBL is a comprehensive instructional framework that inherently allows students to grow in critical skills such as self-awareness, critical thinking, collaboration, responsible decision making, and creativity. It enables students to grow in the skills and dispositions educators want to see in ideal graduates.

2. Theoretically, PBL allows students to apply their content knowledge and understanding or transfer their learning. The PBL unit design provides a clear opportunity for an equal intensity of surface, deep, and transfer levels of learning.

3. When implemented well, PBL promotes equity and is a culturally responsive approach to teaching.

It is because of these three key factors that PBL is worth sustaining. The following sections address each of these factors in more detail.

The First Why

Some schools have done extensive work in developing a graduate profile for their district. The first step in this work is to pose the question, "What are the qualities, skills, and dispositions that we want from the ideal graduates of this school district?" Through the work I do with PBLWorks, I have had the opportunity of posing that question to thousands of educators around the United States since 2010. Not surprisingly, educators' answers to that question are incredibly similar. They are similar from state to state and from elementary teachers to high school teachers. They are similar between schools teaching students in poverty and schools teaching students in privilege. They are similar whether I ask that question in Parramatta, Australia; Loudoun County, Virginia; Texarkana, Arkansas; West Hempstead, New York; or New Hampton, Iowa.

In nearly every such discussion, teachers and administrators state that they want students to have strong skills in the following.

- Collaboration
- Critical thinking
- Problem solving
- Perseverance
- Confidence
- Empathy
- Responsibility
- Cultural responsiveness
- Creativity
- Community mindedness
- Self-awareness
- Self-management

Project-based learning as a comprehensive instructional framework provides intentional opportunities for students to grow in these critical skills and dispositions that we all want in the ideal graduate.

Once site-based teams have consensus on the characteristics and skills they want in the ideal graduate, the next question to pose is, "What are the strategies and activities you implement in your classroom from which you are getting the most impact and skill growth with students?" Responses to this question vary a bit more, especially at the secondary level, when content and instructional strategies become more specialized. However, there are some common patterns in responses among elementary and secondary educators. Typically, these responses include the following.

- Classroom discussions (such as Socratic seminars)
- Student choice in crafting how to demonstrate evidence of learning
- Opportunities for students to set their own goals within the content standards
- Clarity on expectations
- Service-learning projects
- Activities with a real-world connection
- Student choice in reading

- Investigations of provocative questions (such as an inquiry lab in a science classroom)
- Multiple and consistent opportunities for student collaboration
- Direct instruction
- Small-group guided practice

These strategies should fit into project-based learning. When it comes to PBL, you should not abandon successful instructional practices but integrate them within the context of an authentic, real-world challenge. Students should have the opportunity to display or discuss their response to that authentic real-world challenge in the form of a culminating public product. In other words, teachers should incorporate those strategies and activities that are having a high impact into the project-based learning unit.

Some teachers have told me that when they participate in professional development about PBL, they often leave the training feeling like the way they are teaching is wrong. If you are not using PBL as a primary instructional methodology, it does not mean that you are doing something wrong. You should view PBL as a comprehensive instructional framework that, when implemented well, achieves simultaneous learning outcomes for students. When executed well, PBL allows students to grow in their content knowledge as well as the key skills and dispositions we want in ideal graduates.

The Second Why

To understand the second why of PBL, first examine the term *rigor*—a buzzword that educators often throw around. But what does it mean? In his book *Teaching for Transfer: A Guide for Designing Learning With Real-World Application*, Michael McDowell (2021) offers the definitions for several relevant terms in PBL: *rigor, surface-level learning, deep-level learning,* and *transfer.*

- **Rigor:** Rigor is "the equal intensity and integration of surface, deep, and transfer learning" (p. 4). A rigorous unit of study would consist of intentional instructional strategies and assessments targeted at each level of learning—surface, deep, and transfer.

- **Surface-level learning:** This is "the ability for an individual to understand one or more concepts but not the ability to make connections between concepts" (p. 6). An example of surface-level learning would be when students can understand basic facts and critical vocabulary terms.

- **Deep-level learning:** This is "the ability for an individual to relate concepts but not the ability to apply the concepts to one or more contexts" (p. 6). An example of deep-level learning would be when students can determine cause and effect or compare and contrast two different facts.

- **Transfer:** Transfer is "an individual's ability to appropriately apply a concept, skill, or theory within a domain of knowledge to a new context" (p. 6). Transfer is the ultimate goal of education—the deepest level of learning. As you saw at the beginning of this chapter, transfer is the application of knowledge and skills acquired at the surface and deep levels. An example of transfer would be when students can apply their content knowledge and skills to multiple real-world contexts.

To further your understanding of transfer, consider the example eighth-grade social studies unit I feature throughout this book. In this unit, students learn how to conduct historical research through the context of the U.S. Civil War. This anchor unit, called Modern-Day Abolitionists, is an adaptation of a unit I taught in my eighth-grade classroom. So, let's say students are learning about the strategies American abolitionists used in the 1840s and 1850s, and work to apply those strategies to generate social awareness of slavery; they are demonstrating transfer-level learning. Or, better yet, if they are able to apply the persuasive techniques those abolitionists used to generate awareness of a completely different issue (for example, voter registration), that is also an example of transfer.

In looking back on McDowell's (2021) definition of rigor, I would argue that teachers should incorporate this equal intensity of surface, deep, and transfer learning within the context of a unit of study. This is a foundational belief to sustain project-based learning.

In a traditionally designed unit of study, teaching begins with basic knowledge first, and then students learn at a deep level, and hopefully arrive at the transfer level by the end of the unit. In project-based learning, you, the teacher, are held accountable by a driving question written at the transfer level, so you, in theory, must teach content at the transfer level. Figure 1.5 shows a basic comparison of traditional teaching and project-based learning.

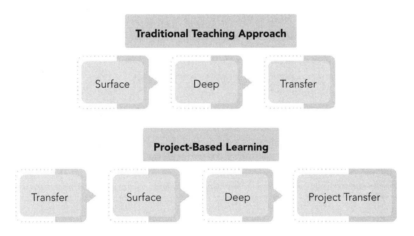

Source: Adapted from McDowell, 2021. Used with permission.

Figure 1.5: Traditional teaching versus project-based learning.

More specifically, a PBL unit begins with a driving question such as *To what extent can we use our knowledge of the past to abolish slavery today?* This driving question is written at the transfer level, so from the very beginning of the unit, students see how the content knowledge they will learn applies in a different, real-world context.

Figure 1.6 (page 18) breaks down all the PBL design elements and what they look like in an exemplary PBL classroom. The entry event is conducted at the transfer level, as well as the driving question. The teacher then conducts direct instruction to build knowledge through minilessons on both key vocabulary and how to research. The minilessons and research are done at the surface level. When students consult outside experts, they ask questions for when they need to demonstrate cause and effect and compare and contrast. The project concludes with students answering the driving question in some sort of public forum. To answer the driving question adequately, students must demonstrate their surface- and deep-level knowledge.

Gold-Standard PBL Design Elements	Definition	What It Looks Like in an Exemplary PBL Classroom
Learning Goals (Key Knowledge, Understanding, and Success Skills, at the center of figure 1.1, page 11)	The project is focused on teaching students key knowledge and understanding derived from standards and success skills, such as critical thinking, collaboration, creativity, and project management.	The number of standards students will learn drives the amount of time the unit takes. The teacher identifies the standards in the form of clear learning intentions (major concepts) and success criteria (daily or weekly learning targets) at each level of complexity (surface, deep, and transfer).
Challenging Problem or Question	The project is based on a meaningful problem or question at the appropriate level of challenge for students, which is focused on an open-ended, engaging driving question.	The teacher writes the driving question at the transfer level and displays it clearly in the classroom. When asked, students can restate it. Students understand the driving question as the context from which they will apply their knowledge and understanding of the content.
Sustained Inquiry	Students generate questions that go to the heart of the content. This process is ongoing throughout the duration of the project. Students use a variety of resources to help them generate more questions and develop their own ideas.	The teacher bases 85 to 95 percent of direct instruction, activities, and strategies on student-generated questions because now students have "bread crumbs" to help them navigate and ask questions at the surface, deep, and transfer levels.
Authenticity	The project has a real-world context; uses real-world processes, tools, and quality standards; makes a real impact; and is connected to students' concerns, interests, and identities.	Students see how the content they are learning transfers to the real world. They understand what occupations are grappling with similar driving questions, scenarios, and challenges. Students have an opportunity to ask questions and receive feedback from outside experts, not just at the end but throughout the unit.
Student Voice and Choice	The project allows students to make their voices heard and implement choices about what they investigate, the products they create, and how they work and use their time (guided by the teacher, as appropriate).	Students have ownership in the process, whether it is choice of a particular role on a collaborative team, choice in the product, or choice in success criteria development in an effort to meet the learning intentions and answer the driving question.
Reflection	The project provides opportunities for students to reflect on what and how they are learning, and on the project's design and implementation.	Students have consistent opportunities to identify where they are in their learning. They have opportunities to journal and partake in a variety of activities in which they are exercising metacognition about their learning.
Critique and Revision	The project includes processes for students to give and receive feedback on their work, in order to revise their ideas and products or conduct further inquiry.	Students are able to identify what exemplars are for their learning intentions and success criteria. Students engage in a variety of feedback protocols *throughout the process*. Throughout the project, students have opportunities to receive feedback from four perspectives: (1) an outside expert who has experience or interest trying to answer a similar driving question, (2) self-critique, (3) peer critique, and (4) the teacher.
Culminating Public Product	The project asks students to demonstrate what they learned by creating a product (artifact, presentation, performance, or event) shared with people beyond the classroom.	Throughout the process, the focus is always on the learning and how the product is a reflection of students' knowledge and understanding of their learning. The public product, however, gives students an opportunity to feel a sense of accountability for their work and understand that it has value beyond the walls of the classroom and beyond themselves.

Source: Adapted from PBLWorks, 2019.

Figure 1.6: An exemplary PBL classroom.

Learning intentions and success criteria are part of what drives a unit (for content and SEL skills). McDowell (2017) states, "Learning intentions are best thought of as brief statements that explicitly describe what students should know and be able to do" (p. 47). These are the significant concepts that typically are learned through a unit of study. "Success criteria specify what students must demonstrate at the surface, deep, and transfer level to ultimately meet learning intentions" (McDowell, 2017, p. 52).

As we define PBL within the context of sustainability, it is imperative to see how McDowell's (2021) definition of rigor connects with PBLWorks' (n.d.) design elements. Connecting these two concepts then helps craft a vision for what exemplary PBL looks like in the classroom.

The Third Why

The third why of PBL is that when done well, PBL promotes equity and is a culturally responsive approach to teaching. In their book *Courageous Conversations About Race: A Field Guide for Achieving Equity in Schools*, authors Glenn E. Singleton and Curtis Linton (2022) define *equity* as "raising the achievement of all students while narrowing the gaps between the highest- and lowest-performing students; and eliminating the racial predictability and disproportionality of which student groups occupy the highest and lowest achievement categories" (p. 46). As stated earlier, the research from the Lucas Foundation finds that PBL has a positive impact on diverse populations, and more than 50 percent of students are from low-income households (Krajcik et al., 2021; Saavedra et al., 2021).

But how, specifically, do educators implement PBL to close these racially divided achievement gaps? In her book *Culturally Responsive Teaching and the Brain*, educator Zaretta Hammond (2015a) lays out an excellent framework for educators to approach culturally responsive teaching. Hammond (2015a) emphasizes that educators should (1) build awareness and knowledge about being a culturally responsive practitioner, (2) build learning partnerships within schools and communities, and (3) build intellective capacity. Two techniques Hammond (2015a) highlights to build intellective capacity are "solve the mystery or real-life problem . . . [and] work on long-term projects" (p. 138). She goes on to suggest that educators "anchor a unit with a place-based learning activity connected to a real-life community issue. Once instruction has been delivered, use the project as an opportunity to apply new skills and knowledge. Select a project that addresses a real-life task" (p. 138).

Additionally, in a research study published in *Educational Psychologist*, Robert J. Jagers, Deborah Rivas-Drake, and Brittney Williams (2019) have this to say about the correlation among PBL, equity, and SEL:

> Student-centered/student-led approaches like PBL . . . are consistent with the core principles of culturally relevant education. However, they are more intentional about positioning students as experts on their own lived experience and capable of working with peers and adults to leverage academic content and skills to devise and iteratively test ways to advance collective well-being. (p. 178)

Both Hammond (2015a) and Jagers and colleagues (2019) state that PBL and long-term, real-world projects can promote culturally responsive teaching practices. This is the third why for PBL.

Summary

Before discussing what makes PBL sustainable, you must have a clear understanding of what PBL is. Project-based learning is not a strategy; it is a comprehensive instructional framework. It promotes growth in important skills; allows for students to grow in surface-, deep-, and transfer-level knowledge; and has been proven to promote equity (Hammond, 2015a; Jagers et al., 2019). PBL is an intentional way to plan, organize, and implement a specific unit of study. For instruction to be considered project-based learning, educators must make a conscious effort of incorporating each design element during the creation and implementation of units of study. To reap all the benefits of PBL, teachers should intentionally incorporate all the seven design elements. If they leave out even one element, it's not that it will result in bad instruction or students won't learn; it's just not project-based learning. Teachers should maintain fidelity to the model of project-based learning.

Questions for Reflection

Individually or in collaborative teams, answer the following questions to reflect on your learning in this chapter.

1. What is your *why* for PBL? Why are you attracted to it compared to other teaching methods?

2. Out of the seven PBL design elements, which one do you find most natural and influential in your planning and implementing, and which one do you find most challenging? Why?

3. What was your most powerful learning experience in school as a student? What made that experience so powerful for you? Did that experience include any of the PBL design elements?

Challenge

With your colleagues, determine the specific qualities, characteristics, and dispositions you want from the ideal graduate. Generate a list and determine the following.

1. How are you defining those qualities, characteristics, and dispositions for students?

2. How are you giving students intentional feedback on their growth in those qualities, characteristics, and dispositions?

3. Which instructional practices and programs that you implement in your classroom have the highest impact on growing those qualities, characteristics, and dispositions (for example, Socratic seminars or a specific lab or simulation)? How might you implement those strategies within the context of a PBL unit?

CHAPTER 2

REVIEWING THE SEVEN PBL
DESIGN ELEMENTS

Prior to focusing on how to *sustain* project-based learning, ensure you have a clear understanding of each of the seven design elements. The PBL design elements lay the foundation for sustaining PBL. These elements are what sets PBL apart from other instructional methods. Making a conscious effort to incorporate all seven design elements helps ensure that students are engaged and powerful learning takes place. Just like cement and steel make up the foundation of a house, the seven design elements lay the foundation for a PBL unit.

This chapter addresses some of the common challenges of each design element and provides some tips, tricks, and examples of how to overcome those challenges. As mentioned in chapter 1 (page 9), I offer an example anchor unit to present a variety of ideas on how to incorporate these design elements.

The Seven Design Elements of PBL

According to PBLWorks (n.d.), seven elements make up the foundation of sustainable PBL: (1) challenging problem or question (the driving question), (2) sustained inquiry, (3) authenticity, (4) student voice and choice, (5) reflection, (6) critique and revision, and (7) culminating public product.

Before examining these seven elements in more detail, I provide some context by showing a completed SPBL unit, the anchor project noted in chapter 1—Modern-Day Abolitionists. As noted previously, I use this anchor unit throughout the book as an example. This overview allows you to see how each element fits into the PBL unit design, including the culminating public product, which is a museum exhibit.

In Indiana, eighth-grade social studies standards include the U.S. Civil War. Figure 2.1 offers a summary of grade 8 social studies standards (that apply to this unit), while figure 2.2 provides the overview of the SPBL anchor unit Modern-Day Abolitionists. The culminating public product is an interactive museum exhibit that will be open to parents, community members, and peers.

Grade 8 U.S. History Growth and Development (to 1877)
Grade 8 students focus on United States history, beginning with a brief review of early history, including the Revolution and Founding Era, and the principles of the United States and Indiana constitutions, as well as other founding documents and their applications to subsequent periods of national history and to civic and political life. Students then study national development, westward expansion, social reform movements, and the Civil War and Reconstruction. Students examine major themes, issues, events, movements, and figures in United States history through the Reconstruction Period (1877) and explore relationships to modern issues and current events.
Students in grade 8 need to experience a variety of teaching and learning strategies. Students are provided practice in thinking and research skills by learning to use the media center, primary documents, and community resources such as historic sites and buildings to identify, evaluate and use appropriate data and reference information. This course also helps students to develop an appreciation of historical thinking skills. Finally, students should demonstrate, through their studies, a commitment to the rights and responsibilities of citizenship in a democratic society.
Indiana Academic Standards for Grade 8 Social Studies are organized around four content areas. The content area standards and the types of learning experiences they provide to students in grade 8 are described below. On the pages that follow, age-appropriate concepts are listed for each standard. Skills for thinking, inquiry, and participation are integrated throughout the standards.

Source: Indiana Department of Education, 2020c, p. 3.

Figure 2.1: Overview of Indiana state standards for grade 8 social studies.

Overview of a PBL Unit: Modern-Day Abolitionists Grade and Subject Area: Eighth Grade Social Studies	
Learning Intention	I can apply the knowledge I gain from historical research on the causes of the U.S. Civil War to create connections and solutions.
Success Criteria	**Surface:** I can define key terms such as *abolitionist, yeoman, popular sovereignty, limited or total war,* and so on. **Deep:** I can compare and contrast the economic causes of slavery in the pre–Civil War era with the economic causes of slavery today. **Transfer:** I can apply my knowledge and understanding of the past and solve a problem that exists today (answer to the driving question).
Driving Question	To what extent can we use our knowledge of the past to abolish slavery today?
Literacy Tasks	**Reading (nonfiction):** Students read the Gettysburg Address (Lincoln, 1863) and excerpts from William Lloyd Garrison's *The Liberator*.

Literacy Tasks	**Reading (fiction):** Students read excerpts from Harriet Beacher Stowe's *Uncle Tom's Cabin* (Stowe, 1852) and a variety of historical fiction texts that students can choose from.
	Writing: Students choose a formal writing assignment. Some choose to write a letter to a politician or a company that had been accused of unfair labor practices. Other students choose to create more of a technical document that displays research comparing and contrasting modern-day slavery with slavery prior to the Civil War.
	Speaking: Students participate in several Socratic seminar discussions in which they are required to use key vocabulary terms as they discuss questions such as, What were Robert E. Lee's feelings toward abolitionists? How would you compare those to the feelings of the factory owner in India today? and If you are not a slaveholder in the United States and a foreign army invades to free slaves held in factories in your country, would you be willing to fight and die for your country?
Outside Experts	Students learn from and receive feedback to their answer to the driving question from a local fair-trade merchant and a community relations director.
Culminating Public Product	Students create an interactive museum in an effort to generate awareness of the issue of modern-day slavery in the textile and agricultural industries. The museum is open to community members, peers, and parents.

Figure 2.2: Overview of a SPBL unit—Modern-Day Abolitionists.

Once students and teachers become more comfortable with the PBL process, then teachers can incorporate all the elements, but adjust them based on their readiness as well as that of their students. The seven essential design elements of PBL units form the foundation for PBL units. The following sections explore each element in detail.

Challenging Problem or Question (The Driving Question)

The *driving question* is the one overarching question that students can refer back to and reflect on throughout the duration of a unit. The driving question goes to the heart of how students apply the content in a real-world context. A great driving question should be a problem or challenge that adults and professionals might be grappling with. Keeping the driving question at the forefront of the learning helps students stay focused. It should be open ended and prompt students to generate questions or *need-to-knows* to begin the sustained-inquiry process. Later in the book, I discuss the specific process for crafting a good driving question.

Sustained Inquiry

Sustained inquiry is a process students use to ask questions and consider what they need to know in order to answer the driving question. As noted previously, in PBL, these student-generated questions are called *need-to-knows*. In an exemplary PBL teacher's classroom, 85 to 95 percent of activities and instruction are based on student need-to-know questions because they go to the heart of the content. Questions are considered need-to-knows when they go beyond just the common questions that students might ask to what students are thinking, "Hey, we need to answer this to answer our driving question." A large portion of sustained inquiry should be focused on students knowing where they are in their learning, where they are going in their learning, and where they have been in their learning.

Sustained inquiry truly is a cyclical process. For example, students receive a driving question or challenge; they consider what they need to know in order to answer that question or address that challenge. The teacher then determines what instructional strategy (for example, direct instruction, class discussion, student research) they are going to use to address the need-to-knows. As students find answers to need-to-knows, new need-to-knows arise, and the process continues. Ideally, students should understand that they cannot go further in their learning if there is a need to know more.

Review figure 1.2 from chapter 1 (page 11). Note the preassessment and postassessment. These are essential to sustained inquiry and the entire unit. Knowing the content of the traditional summative assessment helps scaffold the need-to-know questions and sustained-inquiry process, which can be summarized in the following three steps:

1. Engage students in an entry event with the driving question.

2. Implement the know and need-to-know strategy.

3. Establish clear milestones.

Engage Students in an Entry Event With the Driving Question

The sustained-inquiry process begins with the entry event and driving question. The entry event should involve appealing to a student's emotions, using things such as statistics, pictures, or perhaps an outside expert who is facing a similar challenge or driving question. Regardless of what strategies you use for an entry event, there is one clear way to evaluate their effectiveness. A good entry event can be evaluated based on the quality of need-to-knows that students produce.

Oftentimes, an entry event can include an *entry document*, as shown in figure 2.3. The entry document allows students to read through an introduction of the unit. An entry document could include the driving question, an explanation of the project, and some key outcomes and expectations. The overarching purpose of both the entry event and the entry document is to start the sustained-inquiry process and encourage students to generate need-to-knows that are relevant in answering the driving question.

Indianapolis Children's Museum of History

Dear Participants,

In the 1850s and 1860s, there were an estimated four million slaves in the Southern part of the United States. Slavery had existed since the ancient Romans, and the Southerners were outraged at Northerners who disagreed with slavery. Southerners felt that it was their right to own slaves, and the Northerners were hypocritical as they wore the clothing and used the goods that were produced with slave labor.

Northern abolitionists, such as William Lloyd Garrison and Harriet Beecher Stowe, were able to persuade thousands to oppose slavery. Politicians such as Abraham Lincoln and Henry Clay argued in favor of emancipation against people like Roger Taney and Jefferson Davis. Activists such as Harriet Tubman, Frederick Douglass, and Dred Scot were former slaves who fought for the rights and freedom of slaves.

Slavery led to a great civil war, and despite good military leadership from generals such as Ulysses S. Grant, Robert E. Lee, and William Sherman, it is estimated that some 618,000 Americans were killed. Many causes led to the Civil War in the United States. Classrooms across the country discuss the Civil War, its causes, the key people involved, and why it happened. Sadly, despite this great victory for humanity in 1865, slavery still exists.

As of November of 2021, according to Freetheslaves.net (2021), there are nearly 40.3 million victims of modern slavery globally. This is due to a population explosion in which the world population has tripled and developing countries have had the most growth. Some businesses have taken advantage of developing countries. Rapid social and economic change has taken away urban and community centers that help the underprivileged. Finally, government corruption around the world allows slavery to go unpunished. Unlike in the 1850s, slaves today are not valuable to their owners; instead, these owners see slaves as disposable and do not have them taken care of if they get sick or need food.

It is possible that some products we buy and investments we make are produced with slave labor—some examples might be cocoa from the Ivory Coast, charcoal used to create steel in Brazil, carpets woven in India, and so on. These products end up in our homes.

In 1863, Abraham Lincoln emancipated slaves in the Southern states of the United States. In 1865, the Thirteenth Amendment was ratified, and in 1868, the Fourteenth Amendment was ratified, abolishing all slavery in the United States. Despite this, slavery still exists. As of 2022, at the writing of this book, *slavery* or *forced labor* is defined as any work or service which people are forced to do against their will, under threat of punishment. Almost all slavery practices contain some element of forced labor (antislavery.org, 2021).

Coincidentally, the Indianapolis Children's Museum of History has been looking to increase student awareness of this humanitarian and social issue. The museum wants to create an engaging, popular, and interactive exhibit that is age appropriate and also can be enjoyed by students around the United States whose schools might not be able to afford a trip to Indianapolis. Your exhibit must:

- Be interactive and engaging to educate guests about the social and political causes of the Civil War and the abolitionist movement of the 1850s and 1860s
- Be age appropriate (think upper elementary or middle school)
- Incorporate accurate action research and data
- Gain funding and sponsorship from Indiana businesses and organizations
- Answer the driving question and inspire visitors to become modern-day abolitionists

In summary, the overarching question you are trying to answer is, *To what extent can we use our knowledge of the past to abolish slavery today?* You will present your answer to the driving question to a representative of the Indianapolis Children's Museum of History. Your presentation must be professional and incorporate the use of media and technology. Collaborate, consult experts, and ask questions.

Good luck, and I look forward to hearing your presentations!

Sincerely,

School Programmer

Indianapolis Children's Museum of History

Figure 2.3: Example of an entry document to start the sustained-inquiry process.

Implement the Know and Need-to-Know Strategy

After students have experienced the entry event and received the driving question, ask them what they know about the problem or challenge. This builds confidence and also serves as a gauge of what background knowledge they bring with them. Once the class has completed their knows, have students begin asking what they need to know in order to answer the driving question. Figure 2.4 depicts a scaffolded need-to-know strategy, in which students have three different categories for which to write need-to-knows. Once students have answered the need-to-knows, they move them to the know column. This builds efficacy and confidence in students as well as acknowledges where they have been and where they are going.

To what extent can we use our knowledge of the past to abolish slavery today?			
Know	**Need-to-Know**		
	Key People Involved	**Economic Causes of the Civil War and Slavery**	**Key Historical Events During the Civil War Era**
The North fought against the South.	Who were key abolitionists before and during the Civil War?	Why did the South think slavery was justified?	What were the main Civil War battles?

Figure 2.4: Scaffolded need-to-know strategy.

To truly honor the need-to-knows students generate, carve out intentional time regularly for students to find answer to these questions. The most prevalent need-to-knows warrant some whole-class instructional time. Students can answer minor need-to-knows in smaller groups or individually.

Establish Clear Milestones

The third step in the sustained inquiry is establishing clear milestones. *Milestones* are the key moments or formative checkpoints in the unit. They are important for helping to gauge qualitative evidence of student learning throughout the unit. Because rigor is defined as the equal intensity of surface-, deep-, and transfer-level learning, teachers should generate milestones for each level of complexity: surface, deep, and transfer (McDowell, 2021). Having key milestones is integral not only to project management but also to the sustained-inquiry process.

Surface-, deep-, and transfer-level learning can be fluid within the context of a project. To ensure all learning levels are represented in the unit design and implementation process, intentionally incorporate milestones that provide evidence of learning at all three levels throughout the unit. To that end, during the planning process, teachers should consider the ideal anticipated need-to-knows for each milestone. In other words, for each major milestone, consider the questions you hope students are asking.

This is a great tip, as it aligns the need-to-knows with each milestone and also forces the unit designer to consider each of the three levels of complexity. At the beginning of the project, surface-level milestones and need-to-knows should focus on students' knowing key facts and key vocabulary. Deep-level milestones and need-to-knows should focus on students' comparing and contrasting and determining cause and effect. Finally, transfer-level milestones should focus on students' answering the driving question, applying their learning in a different context, and being able to change the context (not content) of the driving question and still have a strong answer.

Anticipating student need-to-knows for each milestone not only adds integrity to the sustained-inquiry process but also serves as a formative assessment for the three levels of learning (surface, deep, and transfer). You can learn more about anticipated need-to-knows and a tool for planning out milestones in chapter 6 (page 87).

Authenticity

In a popular blog, former chief editor of PBLWorks and PBL pioneer John Larmer (2012) states that "there is a sliding scale of authenticity for projects, which goes from 'not authentic' to 'somewhat authentic' to 'fully authentic.'" A fully authentic PBL unit is when students are addressing or solving a real-world problem or challenge. In a fully authentic PBL unit, students are getting feedback from an outside expert in some fashion before, during, and after the unit. When students are able to get feedback from an expert who has a perspective with the driving question that the teacher might not have, it can make learning more meaningful. Making the project fully authentic allows students to see how the content they are learning is applicable in a real-world context.

Student Voice and Choice

The voice-and-choice element is challenging because, by nature, teachers often feel the need to be in control. They want to have a set routine and set agendas. They can have these things within the context of PBL, but they also have a responsibility to make sure students have ownership of their work. Student ownership can enhance engagement as well as empower students.

If students are all working on different products, that can be more challenging to manage than if they are all working on the same product but with different perspectives. So as we consider the element of voice and choice, and the culminating public product is a museum exhibit, each student could choose an individual role. One student can take the role of the data analysis expert, another can be the content researcher, and another, the community relations expert. Each role has specific responsibilities, but students are all working toward the same culminating public product—a museum exhibit. Figure 2.5 gives an overview of the roles students can take for the unit.

1. Community relations director: The community relations director finds answers to the following questions: How can we market to and create awareness in our community? Who can we get to come to the event? Are there any local or national celebrities who are currently dedicated to the project and could reach a large audience? You must contact a minimum of three people via telephone, email, or formal letter. You will also be responsible for inviting an audience for the final day.

Formal writing assignment—Letter to a senator or corporate executive or other contact person

2. Exhibit designer and technology expert: This person is responsible for researching different museum websites, such as websites of the Indianapolis Children's Museum of History, Conner Prairie, and the National Underground Railroad Freedom Center. You are responsible for utilizing the accessible resources (folding table, laptop) as well as using research and creativity to make the format and design of the display.

Formal writing assignment—Letter to a senator or corporate executive

3. Team leader: The team leader is responsible for helping coach students to meet deadlines, catching them up if they are absent, holding the team accountable to Patrick Lencioni's (2005) team pyramid, and leading the peer team in feedback protocols, such as the Tuning Protocol in figure 8.5 (page 115). You will meet with the teacher on a daily basis to ensure that everyone is clear on instructions and expectations. Although all students will be assessed individually and no team grade will be awarded, the team leader has the important role of ensuring that all parts of the project are being completed and helping with overall organization of the team.

Formal writing assignment—Brochure

4. Data analysis expert: The data analysis expert is responsible for statistical analysis of current slave labor practices in the world. After analyzing the data, you will be responsible for incorporating maps, graphs, and charts into the final exhibit.

Formal writing assignment—Technical document involving graphs, charts, and visuals comparing and contrasting modern-day slavery with slavery in the 1850s

5. Fair-trade researcher: The fair-trade researcher makes connections between slave labor and Northern abolitionists and child labor and modern-day slavery with fair-trade buyers. You are responsible for finding local businesses that buy and sell fair-trade products, such as Whole Foods, Fresh Market, and Trader Joe's. You will also question products that do not promote fair trade (for example, chocolate and coffee).

Formal writing assignment—Letter to a senator or corporate executive or other contact person

Figure 2.5: Example roles for Modern-Day Abolitionist SPBL unit.

Figures 2.6–2.10 (pages 28–32) depict the handouts that one might give students with the specific tasks for each role. Using these roles not only promotes student voice and choice (as students choose their roles), but it also helps manage the process, ensures indivdiual student responsibility, and provides a way to differentiate.

Community Relations Director

Name: _____

Period: _____

I am responsible for the following tasks for my team. (Check all that apply.)

Check	Task
	I displayed community correspondence in the exhibit (for example, letters and emails written).
	I sent emails and made phone calls, inviting community members and parents to attend the museum exhibit event.
	I advertised the museum exhibit event throughout the school and community.
	I sent follow-up correspondence to contacts we did not hear back from.
	I ensured the content portion of the display board met all criteria stated in the rubric.
	I incorporated my book-club book into my section of the museum exhibit.
	I individually completed my section of the exhibit based on the success criteria in the rubric.
	I individually answered the driving question. My answer is clear and thorough and can be applied to real life (for example, encouraging visitors to buy certain fair-trade products and support specific companies and brands that promote fair labor practices).
	I included at least five words from the Civil War core word list in the exhibit.
	Other:
	Other:

You must know the answers to these three questions and be prepared to discuss them with anyone who visits your exhibit.

1. How does modern-day slavery compare to slavery before the Civil War?
2. Harriet Beecher Stowe, Frederick Douglass, Harriet Tubman, and William Lloyd Garrison were all abolitionists. How were the strategies you used similar to or different from the strategies they used?
3. Explain the role you had on the team and the specific contributions you made to the exhibit and the team.

Figure 2.6: Example milestone sheet for the community relations director role.

Visit go.SolutionTree.com/21stcenturyskills for a free reproducible version of this figure.

Exhibit Designer and Technology Expert

Name: _____

Period: _____

I am responsible for the following tasks for my team. (Check all that apply.)

Check	Task
	I ensured all team members had an appropriate amount of space for the exhibit.
	I applied information and ideas I got from other museums' websites and my letter responses to the museum exhibit.
	I saved all electronic data needed for my team's museum exhibit on both a flash drive and Google Drive.
	I ensured my exhibit is interactive, meaning that participants can become involved in some way.
	I ensured the content portion of the display board met all criteria stated in the rubric.
	I incorporated my book-club book into my section of the museum exhibit.
	I individually completed my section of the exhibit based on the success criteria in the rubric.
	I individually answered the driving question. My answer is clear and thorough and can be applied to real life (for example, encouraging visitors to buy certain fair-trade products and support specific companies and brands that promote fair labor practices).
	I included at least five words from the Civil War core word list in the exhibit.
	Other:
	Other:

You must know the answers to these three questions and be prepared to discuss them with anyone who visits your exhibit.

1. How does modern-day slavery compare to slavery before the Civil War?
2. Harriet Beecher Stowe, Frederick Douglass, Harriet Tubman, and William Lloyd Garrison were all abolitionists. How were the strategies you used similar to or different from the strategies they used?
3. Explain the role you had on the team and the specific contributions you made to the exhibit and the team.

Figure 2.7: Example milestone sheet for the exhibit designer and technology expert role.

*Visit **go.SolutionTree.com/21stcenturyskills** for a free reproducible version of this figure.*

Team Leader

Name: _____

Period: _____

I am responsible for the following tasks for my team. (Check all that apply.)

Check	Task
	I provided and organized peer feedback protocols, such as the Tuning Protocol, to my team's exhibit based on the rubric success criteria.
	I ensured that all content requirements were met based on the rubric.
	I displayed the brochure I created as part of the museum exhibit.
	I ensured each member of my team individually answered the driving question.
	I incorporated my book-club book into my section of the museum exhibit.
	I individually answered the driving question. My answer is clear and thorough and can be applied to real life (for example, encouraging visitors to buy certain fair-trade products and support specific companies and brands that promote fair labor practices).
	I individually completed my section of the exhibit based on the success criteria in the rubric.
	I included at least five words from the Civil War core word list in the exhibit.
	Other:
	Other:

You must know the answers to these three questions and be prepared to discuss them with anyone who visits your exhibit.

1. How does modern-day slavery compare to slavery before the Civil War?
2. Harriet Beecher Stowe, Frederick Douglass, Harriet Tubman, and William Lloyd Garrison were all abolitionists. How were the strategies you used similar to or different from the strategies they used?
3. Explain the role you had on the team and the specific contributions you made to the exhibit and the team.

Figure 2.8: Example milestone sheet for the team leader role.

Visit go.SolutionTree.com/21stcenturyskills for a free reproducible version of this figure.

Data Analysis Expert

Name: _____

Period: _____

I am responsible for the following tasks for my team. (Check all that apply.)

Check	Task
	I professionally displayed and explained the charts and graphs I created.
	I saved all electronic data needed for my team's museum exhibit on both a flash drive and Google Drive.
	I clearly posted all resources and references in my team's museum exhibit display board (for example, works cited).
	I ensured the content portion of the display board met all criteria stated in the rubric.
	I incorporated my book-club book into my section of the museum exhibit.
	I individually answered the driving question. My answer is clear and thorough and can be applied to real life (for example, encouraging visitors to buy certain fair-trade products and support specific companies and brands that promote fair labor practices).
	I individually completed my section of the exhibit based on the success criteria in the rubric.
	I included at least five words from the Civil War core word list in the exhibit.
	Other:
	Other:

You must know the answers to these three questions and be prepared to discuss them with anyone who visits your exhibit.

1. How does modern-day slavery compare to slavery before the Civil War?
2. Harriet Beecher Stowe, Frederick Douglass, Harriet Tubman, and William Lloyd Garrison were all abolitionists. How were the strategies you used similar to or different from the strategies they used?
3. Explain the role you had on the team and the specific contributions you made to the exhibit and the team.

Figure 2.9: Example milestone sheet for the data analysis expert role.

Visit go.SolutionTree.com/21stcenturyskills for a free reproducible version of this figure.

Fair-Trade Researcher

Name: _____

Period: _____

I am responsible for the following tasks for my team. (Check all that apply.)

Check	Task
	I clearly displayed the letter I wrote along with any return correspondence I received.
	I have a clear explanation of what fair trade is and how it is different from free trade.
	I made connections between slave labor and Northern abolitionists and child labor and modern-day slavery with fair-trade buyers.
	I ensured the content portion of the display board met all criteria stated in the rubric.
	I incorporated my book-club book into my section of the museum exhibit.
	I individually answered the driving question. My answer is clear and thorough and can be applied to real life(for example, encouraging visitors to buy certain fair-trade products and support specific companies and brands that promote fair labor practices).
	I individually completed my section of the exhibit based on the success criteria in the rubric.
	I included at least five words from the Civil War core word list in the exhibit.
	Other:
	Other:

You must know the answers to these three questions and be prepared to discuss them with anyone who visits your exhibit.

1. How does modern-day slavery compare to slavery before the Civil War?
2. Harriet Beecher Stowe, Frederick Douglass, Harriet Tubman, and William Lloyd Garrison were all abolitionists. How were the strategies you used similar to or different from the strategies they used?
3. Explain the role you had on the team and the specific contributions you made to the exhibit and the team.

Figure 2.10: Example milestone sheet for the fair-trade researcher role.

*Visit **go.SolutionTree.com/21stcenturyskills** for a free reproducible version of this figure.*

Allowing students to have some input in choosing their roles provides them with voice and choice and simultaneously serves as a management tool. You can have role meetings, meaning you can meet with each student or team for a few minutes every period and conduct some guided practice, small-group instruction, or workshops. Allowing students to choose their roles also can promote some goal setting within the context of each role. Additionally, students can have opportunities for flexible grouping where they spend time with their home group (one of each of the five roles represented) and time with their role group (five students with the same role). Both allow opportunities for a high level of student-to-student dialogue on the content.

Having students take on roles such as these can be a valuable strategy to allow some structured voice and choice and help manage the process, but you must be mindful to teach for transfer. The goal with PBL is that students have equal intensity of surface-, deep-, and transfer-level learning. Therefore, when using roles, students should participate in activities such as classroom discussions, debates, and other strategies that force them to learn the perspectives of different roles. Students should be able to answer the driving question through the lens of multiple perspectives, not just one.

Reflection

The essential element of reflection promotes metacognition and critical thinking within the context of a PBL unit. Hattie's (2021) research tells us that self-judgement and reflection has a 0.75 effect size on learning. This is over one and one-half year's growth in one year's time. Whether students keep a journal throughout the process, or you conclude class periods by having students reflect on how what they learned each day connects back to answering the driving question, reflection is imperative to student learning. Students not only can reflect on their growth in content understanding, but also their growth in skills such as self-awareness or social awareness. Once students have completed the PBL unit, you might ask them to reflect on how they answered the driving question or if they would take the same approach if doing the unit again.

Critique and Revision

We know from Hattie's (2021) research that feedback has a high effect size (0.92) on student learning. That is more than two years' growth in one year's time. Throughout a PBL unit, students can receive feedback from four different perspectives, including (1) outside experts, (2) peers, (3) the teacher, and (4) self-critique or self-assessment. No matter which perspective the feedback comes from, it is imperative that students are clear on matching the feedback.

One approach for critique and revision might be to show students an example of a culminating public product (for example, formal writing assignment or model) and discuss what makes the example successful or not so successful. Ensure students understand the expectations for the culminating public product or the success criteria. Then have students use a feedback protocol to provide feedback on the culminating public product. (See example protocols in appendix B, page 141.) Typically, these protocols would be used as a peer critique, but they can also be used to self-critique.

Culminating Public Product

Teachers can measure their teaching effectiveness by examining the quality of work that students produce—both quantitative work, like standardized tests, and qualitative work, like student products. A culminating public product might consist of students presenting in front of outside experts or designing and posting an informational webpage. A culminating public product could mean a community open house or presenting information to parents.

The purpose of a culminating public product is twofold: (1) it provides students with an opportunity to receive feedback from someone who has a unique or insightful perspective; and (2) it increases student accountability for their learning. However, teachers often find it intimidating to display student work for experts, parents, or community members because if the work is poor or lacking, it can reflect badly on the teacher or embarrass the student. Having a public showcase, an exhibition night, or an open house, or having something published, can be overwhelming. Here are a few helpful tips for dealing with culminating public products.

- Create a culture in which students recognize their culminating public product is a reflection of where they are in their learning, and how they have been able to transfer their learning, not of how cool they can make the product look. Allow students opportunities to talk about where they started in their learning and where they are going.

- List key milestones and conduct a dress rehearsal or practice prior to the culminating public product, so you know exactly where students are in their learning at all times. An effective PBL teacher tracks and gauges student progress on each milestone of the unit through informal and formal checkpoints, so when the exhibition night or culminating public product display comes, there are no surprises.

- Recognize and believe in the value of having a culminating public product. Aren't adults more accountable for their work when they know it is going to be displayed in front of others? Having students publicly display work that is of value puts a high level of accountability on students compared to having them work through a series of worksheets. It is possible an outside expert listening to an elementary student's answer to the driving question might apply an idea the student offered in the real world. At the secondary level, an outside expert might be so impressed with a student that they might offer that student a summer internship, or even more. There is tremendous value in having students showcase a culminating public product.

- Start with a public audience with whom you feel comfortable. Consider your friends and relatives who could simply provide students with feedback and perspective that you, the teacher, cannot. PBL teacher and consultant Brian Schoch says it best:

  > Your public audience can be anyone students don't know or anyone who is old (and over twenty-two is old to a student). You don't have to line up a NASA astronaut, and it can be your friend who is an engineer. Once you're comfortable bringing people to your classroom, you can start to branch out a little. (B. Schoch, personal communication, March 4, 2020)

No question, implementing the design elements of PBL can be challenging. However, do not allow fear of these elements to hinder your implementing what might be the most valuable learning experience for students.

Perspectives From the Field: Brian Schoch
Working With Outside Experts in Your Classroom

Something I do in my classroom that is very impactful for students (and I greatly enjoy too) is collaborating with professionals from the business community. Each time, I find my students have a greater level of engagement, enjoyment, and purpose while working on their projects. Truthfully, it makes my job as a teacher easier and more fulfilling.

Yet, as a PBL consultant and coach, oftentimes when I bring up the idea of bringing non-educators into the classroom, it is met with passive resistance. I say *passive* resistance because no one ever says, "That's a bad idea"; however, I am often asked, "Is it still PBL if I just keep this in my classroom? Do I *have to* have a public audience?"

To me, utilizing business and industry in my classroom is not a "have to"—it's a "get to." You get to enhance the relevance of your project. You get to watch students present to someone who works in this area. You get to see the connection of your classroom to potential career paths.

With this in mind, here are a few tips to make the most of your engagement with outside experts in your classroom.

Who should I contact? Oftentimes, teachers think they need to have a contact at NASA or a senator be their outside expert. Though it's great to reach for the stars, sometimes your neighbor who is an engineer is just as impactful. If you are leery of using an outside expert, start with people you know—for example, neighbors, friends, college roommates, and community members. You will be a bit more comfortable working with someone you know initially. Then you can branch out and expand your contact list. Look for energetic people who seem like they'd enjoy working with students. That's as important as, if not more important than, their job title.

How or when should I utilize them? Think beyond the guest speaker to start the unit. (It takes a pretty remarkable guest speaker to hold a group of students' attention beyond ten minutes.) Have a role for them in your project. Are they posing the challenge for the students? Are they a consultant the students meet with during the project? Do they provide feedback at the end of the project? I find that simply asking the question, "How can I best utilize you for this project?" is a great conversation starter and leads to many ideas that I hadn't considered.

What if some students aren't behaving? Won't that reflect poorly on me, the teacher? I've found that my students are more engaged and behave their best when I have outside experts in my classroom. In twenty-plus years in education, I've never had someone tell me, "These students didn't behave; I won't come back." To the contrary, the vast majority of the time, the outside experts ask if they can help out again in the future. Having done this for a while, I have a great group of contacts that are almost always willing to help out in whatever way they can. Students have done in-class projects over and over again. It's time to take a chance. Push yourself out of your comfort zone a little bit; push your students a little bit. You'll be glad you did.

(B. Schoch, high school business teacher, PBL consultant, and coach; personal communication, May 19, 2020)

The PBL Equalizer

Before the time of wireless Bluetooth speakers and smartphones, home stereos were huge. The bigger the speakers, the better. Often, the stereos had equalizers on them where you could adjust each sound aspect individually. You could adjust the bass, treble, fade, tone, and so on. For some songs, cranking up the bass sounded amazing. Other songs, however, needed more treble. The equalizer allowed the owner to customize the sound to one's exact specification.

We can use the analogy of a stereo equalizer to consider the seven PBL design elements. As shown in figure 2.11 (page 36), the concept of a PBL equalizer allows teachers to design units of study with varying degrees of PBL elements in them. Teachers can decide to crank up or turn down specific elements, depending on context, content, and comfort level.

Not only can you use the PBL equalizer to determine how you might prioritize the design elements, but you also can use it to determine your own comfort level with them. If you were asked to rank the seven design elements from most challenging to least challenging, how would you rank them and why? Frequently, those beginning their PBL journey rank voice and choice, sustained inquiry, and culminating public product as more challenging than the other elements. Note that these elements are absolutely essential to PBL, but each of them can be a bit intimidating. As a result, your first few units might look a bit like the PBL equalizer in figure 2.12 (page 37).

The Driving Question	Student Voice and Choice	Reflection	Critique and Revision	Sustained Inquiry	Authenticity	Culminating Public Product
The teacher writes the driving question at the transfer level using a sentence stem such as: • To what extent . . . ? • Who . . . ? • Where . . . ? • When . . . . ?	Students have significant ownership in determining their goals, challenges, solutions, and products. Student work is centered on a clear learning intention and success criteria.	Students participate in individual metacognition, such as journaling on a daily basis throughout the unit.	Students receive specific feedback throughout the unit on both content and skills through or from the following, and they use a variety of protocols to improve their work. • Self-reflection • Peers • Outside experts • The teacher	Eighty-five to 90 percent of activities and instruction are based on student need-to-know questions because they go to the heart of the content.	The product or solution has a direct impact and use in the real world. Students take action to make a positive impact on their community or world.	Students' concepts, ideas, or aspects of their ideas in their public products are so useful that they are applied and actually used by professionals or people outside the classroom.
High — Low	High — Low	High — Low	High — Low	High — Low	High — Low	High — Low
The teacher writes the driving question at the surface level using a sentence stem such as: • How . . . ? • What . . . ?	The teacher structures the unit so they primarily determine the goals, challenges, solutions, and products.	The teacher asks students occasional reflective questions during activities such as warm-ups or exit slips.	The teacher gives students general feedback throughout the unit, not necessarily using protocols and not giving it from all four perspectives (listed previously).	Ten to 15 percent of activities and instruction are based on student need-to-know questions.	The PBL unit experience simulates what might happen in the real world.	The teacher asks students to present to the class.

Source: Adapted from © 2021 by Kristyn A. Kamps. Used with permission.

Figure 2.11: The PBL equalizer.

The Driving Question	Student Voice and Choice	Reflection	Critique and Revision	Sustained Inquiry	Authenticity	Culminating Public Product
The teacher writes the driving question at the transfer level using a sentence stem such as: • To what extent . . . ? • Who . . . ? • Where . . . ? • When . . . ?	Students have significant ownership in determining their goals, challenges, solutions, and products. Student work is centered on a clear learning intention and success criteria.	Students participate in individual metacognition such as journaling on a daily basis throughout the unit.	Students receive specific feedback throughout the unit on both content and skills through or from the following, and they use a variety of protocols to improve their work. • Self-reflection • Peers • Outside experts • The teacher	Eighty-five to 90 percent of activities and instruction are based on student need-to-know questions because they go to the heart of the content.	The product or solution has a direct impact and use in the real world. Students take action to make a positive impact on their community or world.	Students' concepts, ideas, or aspects of their ideas in their public products are so useful that they are applied and actually used by professionals or people outside the classroom.
High — Low	High — Low	High — Low	High — Low	High — Low	High — Low	High — Low
The teacher writes the driving question at the surface level using a sentence stem such as: • How . . . ? • What . . . ?	The teacher structures the unit so they primarily determine the goals, challenges, solutions, and products.	The teacher asks students occasional reflective questions during activities such as warm-ups or exit slips.	The teacher gives students general feedback throughout the unit, not necessarily using protocols and not giving it from all four perspectives (listed previously).	Ten to 15 percent of activities and instruction are based on student need-to-know questions.	The experience simulates what might happen in the real world.	The teacher asks students to present to the class.

Source: Adapted from © 2021 by Kristyn A. Kamps. Used with permission.

Figure 2.12: The adjusted PBL equalizer.

Summary

Each of the seven PBL design elements pose their own challenges. While one design element might be challenging to one teacher, it might come naturally to another teacher. Consider looking at the elements as a stereo equalizer. Do not let one or two elements deter you from implementing PBL. Try to incorporate all seven elements in your PBL units, but to varying degrees. All of them have the potential to enhance student learning. Remember that PBL is about learning during the unit, not the final culminating public product. The product should be evidence of where students are, where they have been, and where they are going in their learning.

Questions for Reflection

Individually or in collaborative teams, answer the following questions to reflect on your learning in this chapter.

1. Which element do you find comes most naturally, and which one do you find most challenging? Explain your answer.

2. When you were a student, what were some occasions when you experienced having voice and choice, engaging in sustained inquiry, or producing a culminating public product? Did any of these elements lead to powerful learning experiences for you? Why or why not?

3. In what ways might you have students produce key milestones throughout the process connected to voice and choice, sustained inquiry, and a culminating public product?

Challenge

Consider how you might implement the elements you find most challenging. If you are already implementing one or all of these elements, consider how you might increase the degree to which you apply them.

CHAPTER 3

MAINTAINING A SUSTAINABLE RELATIONSHIP WITH PROJECT-BASED LEARNING

Now that we have laid the foundation and explained the purpose and benefits of project-based learning, it's time to discuss a significant focus of this book—sustainability. This chapter presents some of the challenges of making PBL sustainable in schools. You will explore some pitfalls that lead to a lack of PBL sustainability and then consider specific approaches to support sustainability. But first, let's look at a hypothetical case study of Harrison School District. As you read, think about how you might relate to the Harrison School District experience.

Case Study: Harrison School District

Harrison School District is an urban district located in the heart of the Rust Belt, a region of the Northeastern and Midwestern United States that has experienced industrial decline since the 1980s. The city of Harrison is made up of about one hundred thousand citizens. In the 1950s, Harrison was a thriving city that consisted mostly of working professionals. These professionals had high-wage jobs and amazing retirement pensions. The majority of these high-wage jobs were in the large automobile factories scattered around the city. Two major car-manufacturing plants were based in the town. There was another plant that manufactured the stereos that went into the automobiles. During this era, weekend nights spent around the courthouse square were like a scene from a movie. People mingled on the sidewalks as convertibles rolled by. Buildings looked clean and shiny.

Fast-forward forty years, and Harrison was much different. The factories were all gone, and the city turned to the local school district to empower and equip students with the knowledge and skills needed for the 21st century. Conversations around new methods of teaching and learning created a buzz among local politicians and school administrators. "We want to provide students with a learning experience that engages them to solve real-world problems." The community also

continued ▶

called on a greater devotion to equity in the curriculum. Test score data indicated that students of color were not performing as well on standardized tests as White students. In addition, student surveys indicated that a decent percentage of students of color did not feel as comfortable at school as White students.

The district administration shopped around several curriculum ideas and ultimately landed on project-based learning. The question that the Harrison School District administrators challenged one another with was, "How can we get all teachers to implement project-based learning?" Harrison School District received a large grant for professional development, and a plan was put in place to train all 357 middle school and high school teachers across the district in PBL. The district invested $150,000 in professional development. All 357 teachers plus administrators went through a three-day introductory workshop in which they designed a PBL unit. The trainings were engaging and thoughtful and modeled a variety of best practices in PBL planning and implementation. District administrators mandated that all teachers who attended the training would be expected to implement one PBL unit that year, two PBL units the following year, and four PBL units the third year after training.

Fast-forward three years. A very small number of teachers were implementing PBL units throughout the district. Significant amounts of time, money, and resources were spent on Harrison's PBL initiative. This was frustrating to teachers, administrators, and the community. The problem with Harrison School District's plan was that the district did not approach PBL implementation with a vision for sustainability.

The Importance of Sustainability

As you reflect on the hypothetical case study featuring Harrison School District, you will recognize why sustainability is so important. Consider the time and resources invested into project-based learning. All the teachers were pulled out of school for three days of valuable instructional time with the hope that the initiative would be implemented. The administration's intentions were good, as they wanted to provide students with more meaningful learning experiences. However, they did not have a long-term vision that was sustainable.

Harrison School District was facing three issues.

1. It was mandating PBL from the top down.

2. It was not incorporating school-improvement plans or leveraging early adopters.

3. It was asking the wrong questions.

Let's unpack each of these issues in the following sections and reflect on how these lessons might impact your own work with PBL.

Mandating PBL From the Top Down

Harrison School District's story is not uncommon when it comes to PBL implementation. The administrators of Harrison School District had good intentions. They wanted to provide students with a relevant, rigorous, and engaging curriculum. However, they could have taken more initiative up front in gathering teacher input. Teachers could have had more ownership in the process instead of following a top-down mandate.

Too often, administrators attend a conference, read a book, or find success doing certain things that work for them in their own classrooms and believe their schools should implement those ideas. There are two significant problems with this thinking.

1. Teaching is personal.

2. Forcing engagement can lead to teacher resistance.

Teaching Is Personal

There is an art to teaching. Just as great artists determine how to paint their canvas, great teachers must have some autonomy over their teaching. Anyone who has been a substitute teacher or implemented someone else's lesson plans knows that envisioning how to implement plans you haven't authored or don't have ownership in can be difficult. It is like a cover band playing a song written by another artist. Sure, it might do OK, but no matter how hard the cover band tries, it cannot be the same as the original artist. Teaching is an art. The teacher is an artist, and teaching flourishes when the teacher is allowed some autonomy and ownership when designing and implementing their art. This is why when we discuss PBL, there are certain nonnegotiables to consider. These nonnegotiables add guidance and structure. At the same time, you should feel empowered to design and implement a PBL unit the way that you see fit.

Forcing Engagement Can Lead to Resistance

The artist needs some autonomy to paint their canvas, just like a teacher needs some autonomy to design and implement their PBL unit. Educational author Phillip C. Schlechty (2001) argues that there are different levels of engagement. Schlechty (2001) directs the levels of engagement toward student engagement, but these same levels can apply to teachers.

As you view Schlechty's (2001) levels of engagement, consider them through two lenses—that of a student (in the classroom) and that of a teacher (pertaining to professional development).

Authentic engagement: The task, activity, or work the student is assigned or encouraged to undertake is associated with a result or outcome that has clear meaning and relatively immediate value to the student.

Ritual engagement: The immediate end of the assigned work has little or no inherent meaning or direct value to the student, but the student associates it with extrinsic outcomes and results that are of value.

Passive compliance: The student is willing to expend whatever effort is needed to avoid negative consequences, although he or she sees little meaning in the tasks assigned or the consequences of doing those tasks.

Retreatism: The student is disengaged from the tasks, expends no energy in attempting to comply with the demands of the tasks, but does not act in ways that disrupt others and does not try to substitute other activities for the assigned task.

Rebellion: The student summarily refuses to do the task, acts in ways that disrupt others, or attempts to substitute tasks and activities to which he or she is committed in lieu of those assigned or supported by the school and by the teacher. (pp. 65–66)

Educators should reflect on Schlechty's (2001) levels of engagement as they pertain to students in their classrooms, and school professional development leaders should reflect on these levels of engagement for teachers. If there is a top-down mandate such as, "All teachers will implement project-based learning," the majority of teachers will implement PBL in an effort to comply. PBL, when implemented to comply with a top-down mandate, has the potential to be detrimental to student learning. If you force artists to perform a song that they do not want to perform, it will not sound as pure and meaningful as a song they feel passionate about.

Regardless of the professional development structure you provide in your school, note that you should never present it as being about fidelity to a specific PBL model. Your goal is to give teachers reasons to feel passionate about PBL. So instead, when rolling out PBL, professional development should be about asking fundamental questions. Following are some questions that help increase teacher and administrator consciousness as to the *why* of implementing more authentic learning experiences.

- In what ways are you intentionally defining and growing the qualities and skills we want from the ideal graduate?

- How do you define *rigor*, and what evidence of that type of learning exists in your classroom?

- Are students gaining not only surface- and deep-level understanding but also transfer-level understanding of the content? Do they understand how to apply the content in the real world or in multiple contexts?

- What percentage of the time are you discussing quality student work (formal writing assignments, products, and so on)?

- If you were to survey students on whether they can see how to apply the content they are learning, what might they say?

It's possible that educators can answer these questions about participating in PBL. However, the end goal for student learning is not PBL. The end goal is that students leave high school with the skills, dispositions, and characteristics that we want from the ideal graduate. Whatever those skills and dispositions are, that is the *why*—the ultimate goal and destination. The way must always be about learning. A mistake I have made in the past is making PBL about the *why*, but PBL is the *how*. Educators might turn away from PBL if you make it about the methodology and not about evidence of student learning.

Not Incorporating School-Improvement Plans or Leveraging Early Adopters

I would rather work in a school where a few teachers were authentically engaged in implementing project-based learning and focused on using it as a methodology to enhance learning than work in a school where all teachers were passively compliant in their opinion and PBL implementation.

If PBL is a professional development initiative in a school, it should be because it is directly tied to the school-improvement plan and a means to accomplish the ultimate goal laid out in the school-improvement plan to enhance student learning.

Once you have a clear school-improvement plan or mission statement that promotes authentic learning through PBL, the next step is to leverage early adopters. When leading a PBL initiative, start with teachers who are genuinely interested and willing to implement the plan. These are the early adopters. For example, if you have a school-improvement plan or mission statement that sounds anything remotely like one of the following bullet points, consider restructuring your monthly faculty meetings and allowing conference-style choices for teachers.

- We will provide real-world, hands-on experiences for students.

- We will provide students with opportunities to determine their professional passions.

- We will provide students with opportunities to be global citizens.

Figure 3.1 provides an example three-year professional development plan for school improvement, which allows teachers choice in what they want to learn. Note that all the choices are in direct alignment to the school improvement goals. To further explain the example in figure 3.1, teachers chose one of the professional development topics, met once per month, and focused on that topic for the duration of the school year. Providing choice generates opportunities for deeper learning.

School-Improvement Goals

1. We will provide real-world, hands-on learning to help students see the connections between their school experience and future experiences they will have after graduation.
2. We will cultivate a school environment to be safe and inclusive for all students.

Year 1 Choices	Year 2 Choices	Year 3 Choices
- Technology Integration - Project-Based Learning - Culturally Responsive Teaching - Understanding by Design - Differentiation	- Technology Integration 101 - Technology Integration 201 - Project-Based Learning 101 - Project-Based Learning 201 - Culturally Responsive Teaching 101 - Culturally Responsive Teaching 201 - Differentiation	- Project-Based Learning 301 - Culturally Responsive Teaching 301 - Others based on teacher interests and needs

Appropriate Steps for the Process

1. School staff take a survey and choose the strand they are most interested in. For each session on each strand, administration clearly communicates that all these strands are under the umbrella of the two school-improvement goals.
2. Beyond the strategies and methods being taught, administration sets an expectation to focus on evidence of the impact on learning.
3. Both planning artifacts and student learning artifacts must be consistently discussed and shared within each professional development meeting strand.
4. Teachers who have experience in a particular strand should plan, lead, or co-lead sessions. These teacher leaders should receive a reasonable amount of time to plan each session.
5. Staff should receive feedback from one another or from the facilitator after every session.

Figure 3.1: Three-year professional development example.

The example in figure 3.1 is appropriate for a large school. For a smaller school, it might be more appropriate to restructure the options. For example, you might not offer as many choices, as the strands should be large enough that there can be a high level of teacher-to-teacher dialogue. This might be challenging to do with only a few teachers in each strand. No matter the school size, a common mistake would be to always focus on the strategy and not on student learning. Another mistake would be not allowing teachers to lead professional development or choose their topic.

The goal of professional development should not focus on implementation of a specific method or model. The goal should focus on evidence of student growth in knowledge and skills. At the same time, as educators, we have a responsibility to refine and perfect our craft. Sometimes, learning can be like exercising. You know it's good for you and you need to do it, but while you're in the middle of it, it's not fun. Afterward, however, you feel great. Setting a school-improvement plan with a clear professional development structure allowing for early adopters to implement PBL can lead to authentic engagement for teachers and meaningful learning experiences for students. Ultimately, it promotes a sustainable relationship with PBL.

Asking the Wrong Questions

You may have noticed that a common theme to sustaining PBL is asking the right questions. Harrison School District administrators asked the wrong questions. Harrison School District administrators were attracted to PBL because of the real-world application. Right away, they asked, "How can we get all teachers to implement project-based learning?" This is the wrong question, because it is about trying to get teacher compliance around a specific instructional approach. The question should *always* be about enhancing learning. If the questions are about the fidelity of implementation, then the priority is on the pedagogy and not the learning. If students are not learning, there is no reason to stay faithful to PBL's seven design elements.

To understand how Harrison School District was asking the wrong questions, it is important to understand the evolution of a district's relationship with PBL. Figure 3.2 shows this evolution through the metaphors of flirting, dating, engaged, and married.

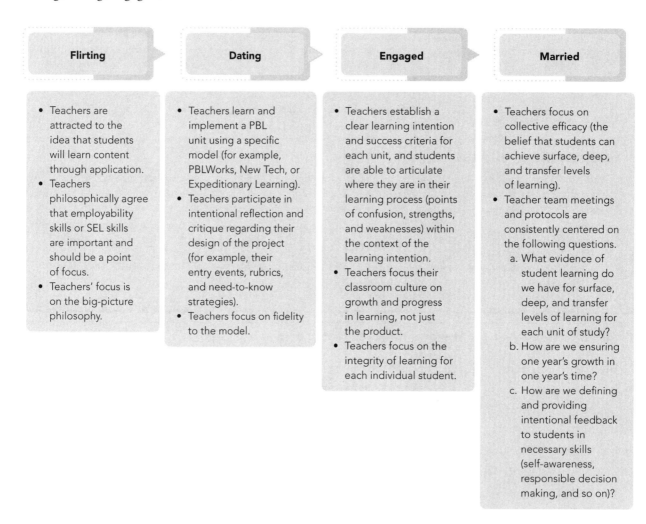

Flirting	Dating	Engaged	Married

• Teachers are attracted to the idea that students will learn content through application.
• Teachers philosophically agree that employability skills or SEL skills are important and should be a point of focus.
• Teachers' focus is on the big-picture philosophy.
	• Teachers learn and implement a PBL unit using a specific model (for example, PBLWorks, New Tech, or Expeditionary Learning).
	• Teachers participate in intentional reflection and critique regarding their design of the project (for example, their entry events, rubrics, and need-to-know strategies).
	• Teachers focus on fidelity to the model.
		• Teachers establish a clear learning intention and success criteria for each unit, and students are able to articulate where they are in their learning process (points of confusion, strengths, and weaknesses) within the context of the learning intention.
		• Teachers focus their classroom culture on growth and progress in learning, not just the product.
		• Teachers focus on the integrity of learning for each individual student.
			• Teachers focus on collective efficacy (the belief that students can achieve surface, deep, and transfer levels of learning).
			• Teacher team meetings and protocols are consistently centered on the following questions.
			  a. What evidence of student learning do we have for surface, deep, and transfer levels of learning for each unit of study?
			  b. How are we ensuring one year's growth in one year's time?
			  c. How are we defining and providing intentional feedback to students in necessary skills (self-awareness, responsible decision making, and so on)?

Source: Adapted from © 2021 by Gavin Hays. Used with permission.

Figure 3.2: Evolution of a district's relationship with PBL.

Figure 3.2 illustrates a district's need to evolve from attempting PBL implementation with complete fidelity to maintaining PBL's integrity as a means to student learning and growth. If you focus on implementation fidelity, at best, you will only "date" PBL. If you want to "marry" PBL, or look at it as a sustainable methodology, the key questions you pose should focus on student learning, not teacher compliance.

Implementation of PBL for Sustainability

Harrison School District should have approached PBL in a way to ensure sustainability. *Sustainable PBL* refers to a process in which teachers have an equal commitment to the following.

- Using the PBL design elements as an instructional framework for planning and implementing units of study

- Identifying and assessing both key academic concepts and social and emotional concepts

- Regularly meeting in teacher teams using protocols for action research, and discussing the following three SPBL questions:

    1. How do you ensure at least one year's growth in one year's time?

    2. How do you ensure an equal intensity of surface-, deep-, and transfer-level learning for each unit of study?

    3. How do you define SEL skills and provide intentional feedback to students on their growth in both content knowledge and SEL skills?

There are aspects of the SPBL process that are nonnegotiable, while some aspects are negotiable. Table 3.1 provides some examples of nonnegotiable and negotiable aspects of SPBL.

TABLE 3.1: Nonnegotiable and Negotiable Aspects of SPBL

Nonnegotiable Aspects of SPBL	Negotiable Aspects of SPBL
An equal commitment to content learning intentions and success criteria and to SEL learning intentions and success criteria	How you determine learning intentions and success criteria
An equal intensity of surface-, deep-, and transfer-level success criteria for both academic and SEL tasks and assessments	What strategies and tasks you use to accomplish equal intensity
A commitment by teacher teams to action research focused on the three sustainable PBL questions: (1) How do you ensure at least one year's growth in one year's time? (2) How do you ensure an equal intensity of surface-, deep-, and transfer-level learning for each unit of study? and (3) How do you define and provide intentional feedback to students on their growth in both content knowledge and SEL skills?	What protocols you use during the action research process

continued ▶

Nonnegotiable Aspects of SPBL	Negotiable Aspects of SPBL
A conscious effort to incorporate at least some of the PBL design elements in each unit throughout the year (and a commitment to doing at least one unit per year with all PBL design elements)	The degree to which you incorporate the PBL design elements and the number of full PBL units you implement (strong encouragement to do at least one, though)
A commitment to using protocols during teacher collaboration time	What protocols you use
A focus on developing assessment-capable learners, meaning students can identify where they are, where they have been, and where they are going in their learning. Ideally, students are familiar with the terms surface, deep, and transfer to describe their learning.	Not applicable
A goal of growth for both students and teachers	The aspects in which you grow (for example, PBL, action research, protocols, content understanding, and so on)

Visit **go.SolutionTree.com/21stcenturyskills** for a free reproducible version of this table.

As you begin thinking about how to make PBL sustainable, remember to keep these nonnegotiable and negotiable aspects in mind. Remember, it is called PBL because it is an ongoing learning process for both students and educators. Students will grow in their academic knowledge and SEL skills, and teachers and administrators will develop their collaboration skills through action research.

Traditional PBL Versus Sustainable PBL

Several factors set sustainable PBL apart from traditional PBL. These factors include:

1. SPBL applies John Hattie's research to emphasize and grow teacher collective efficacy through goal setting and intentional teacher action research focused on evidence of student learning. This is part of the SPBL process, but not inherently a part of planning and implementing a traditional PBL unit. Working in collaborative teams not only grows teacher efficacy, but the team provides support and accountability to focusing on student learning outcomes.

2. SPBL places an equal emphasis on students growing in an SEL skill as it does content knowledge. In SPBL, teachers design an intentional learning intention, success criteria, and tasks centered around both an SEL skill and a content standard. In traditional PBL, an SEL skill might be addressed, or mentioned, but not in as intentional a fashion as in an SPBL unit. This further justifies the amount of time spent on a longer-term unit as students have clear and equally emphasized simultaneous learning outcomes in both a content application and growth in a specific SEL skill.

3. SPBL includes planning the unit using the traditional seven PBL design elements (the driving question, voice and choice, reflection, critique and revision, sustained inquiry,

authenticity, culminating public product). However, SPBL emphasizes going beyond the design elements and focusing on clear evidence of student learning at three levels: (1) surface, (2) deep, and (3) transfer.

4. The SPBL approach is influenced by McDowell's (2017) perspective in *Rigorous PBL by Design*. The SPBL planning template asks unit designers to plan learning intentions and driving questions at the transfer level in a way that allows applications to various contexts. For example, if the learning intention focuses on research, the context for the first year the SPBL unit is implemented might be students conducting research on childhood obesity. The next year, the teacher might change the context from childhood obesity to climate change. The learning intention stays the same (research), but the context changes. This makes units reusable, as the teacher can simply change the contexts of their milestones, assessments, and tasks; they do not have to recreate the unit from scratch. This not only makes the time spent planning more justifiable for the teacher, but focusing on the learning intention void of context helps students see how the skill of research can be applied to multiple contexts, not just one. This approach is different than traditional PBL, as it is likely students are only seeing how to apply learning to one context.

5. SPBL encourages teachers to infuse high-impact tasks and strategies within the context of the SPBL unit (see figure 1.4, page 14, for some of Hattie's high-impact strategies). Traditional PBL does not focus on the intentional use of research-based, high-impact strategies.

6. Figure 3.3 shows a Venn diagram of the three most important components of SPBL. These are what make PBL *sustainable*: (1) student growth in social and emotional learning, (2) deep conversations about learning through teacher action research, and (3) student academic growth through project-based learning.

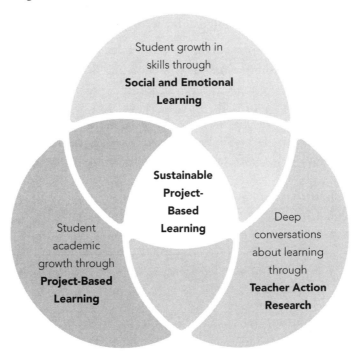

Source: © 2021 by Christian Elden. Used with permission.

Figure 3.3: SPBL Venn diagram.

Teaching is an art, but all artists have some level of guidance and structure. Artists must work in the right conditions to be inspired and successful. The same holds true for educators. As an educator, you must have some guidance and some structure. You must have the conditions to be successful. When it comes to PBL there is a fine line between having guidance and structure and losing ownership of the PBL process. Passive compliance occurs when teachers feel like they must have complete fidelity to a model. Authentic engagement occurs when teachers receive examples and open-ended questions, and have the opportunity to make the art of teaching their own. In order for PBL to be sustainable, planning and implementation should address the three SPBL questions from the previous section and be nonnegotiable on the principles listed in table 3.1 (page 45).

Common Errors in Sustainability

Within the context of a PBL unit, teachers should incorporate influences that have high effect sizes according to Hattie's research (Visible Learning Meta[X], n.d.). This research shines a light on some weaknesses of PBL. For example, when designing and implementing a PBL unit, teachers must be explicitly clear with students regarding the learning intentions (major concepts) and success criteria (daily or weekly learning targets) because teacher clarity has a 0.84 effect size, while self-reported grades have a 1.33 effect size (Visible Learning Meta[X], n.d.). This means students need to be able to identify where they are in their learning, where they have been in their learning, and where they are going in their learning. They should be able to do more than merely restate the driving question or regurgitate the context of a PBL unit. Too often, it gets exciting to think of an authentic context for a project or product, and the content gets lost. You can address a lack of clarity by ensuring that the learning intentions are absolutely clear for students.

Adding an authentic context is an essential element of PBL. However, ensuring that students have a clear understanding of what the content is and how the context leads to the application of that content is more important. In a PBL unit, students should know precisely what the learning intention is, as well as the success criteria, which should be at the surface, deep, and transfer levels of learning.

By being this explicitly clear, teachers help students focus on the *learning* and not the context or the product. In other words, a common error in PBL is that students focus on the context or the product more than the learning goal or application of the learning standard. A clear learning intention also provides students with a greater opportunity to be capable of self-assessment, as they can identify where they are in their learning (surface, deep, or transfer) based on the success criteria. They can say, "I am at the surface level of learning because I am still learning key vocabulary," or "I can compare and contrast the economies of the North and the South, so I am at the deep level."

A common misconception about PBL is people confuse giving students voice and choice with allotting them independent work time for an independent study. Project-based learning is not an independent study (see figure 3.4). If, in fact, PBL is too open ended, and the learning intentions and success criteria are unclear, students might misunderstand the content and walk away unaware of where they are in their learning as it relates to that content. Be intentional about having clear learning intentions and success criteria to help prevent students from getting too blinded by the context instead of being clear about the content.

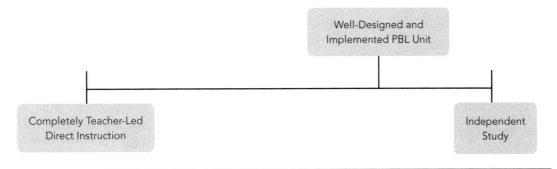

Figure 3.4: Where PBL falls between direct instruction and independent study.

Project-based learning should allow for student voice and choice, but also be based on formative assessments, and teachers should be adaptive and aware of when they need to implement direct instruction and guided practice.

What Makes a PBL Unit Sustainable

As noted previously, we will be using an anchor unit as an example throughout this book—an eighth grade social studies unit called Modern-Day Abolitionists. Figure 3.5 (page 50) is an example of a completed SPBL unit template for Modern-Day Abolitionists. The template is adapted from a template in McDowell's (2017) *Rigorous PBL by Design*. We will unpack this template stage by stage and step by step. At first glance, you should see why this version of PBL is sustainable, considering the following three factors.

The emphasis is on the learning, not the context or the product. The learning intentions and success criteria are clearly established.

1. It integrates the SEL skill directly into the unit. There is an equal value placed on the SEL skill and the content skill.

2. Although thorough, this planning template is meant to be practical for teachers to use as a planning tool.

3. A PBL unit can be overwhelming to plan, so teachers might think the "juice is not worth the squeeze." By adding both greater clarity and integrating SEL skills into the unit, it makes the juice worth the squeeze.

Stage 1: Create a learning intention for both academic content and SEL (a major concept for the unit and a Collaborative for Academic, Social, and Emotional Learning [CASEL] competency).

1. Content learning intention: I can apply the knowledge I gain from historical research on the causes of the U.S. Civil War to create connections and solutions (8.1.11, 8.1.20, 8.1.21, 8.1.22, 8.1.23, 8.1.24, 8.1.25, 8.4.2, 8.4.3, LH.1, LH.2, LH.3, LH.4, LH.5, LH.6, LH.7).

2. SEL learning intention (social awareness): I can present the perspective of another race on an issue of discrimination.

Stage 2: Develop content and SEL success criteria for each level of learning (daily learning goals).

You could have multiple goals; they should be written without context or specificity.

Surface-Level Success Criteria for Content	Deep-Level Success Criteria for Content	Transfer-Level Success Criteria for Content
I can define key terms such as *abolitionist, yeoman, popular sovereignty, limited* or *total war,* and so on.	I can compare and contrast the economic causes of slavery in the pre–Civil War era with the economic causes of slavery today.	I can apply my knowledge and understanding of the past and solve a problem that exists today (answer to the driving question).
Surface-Level Success Criteria for SEL	**Deep-Level Success Criteria for SEL**	**Transfer-Level Success Criteria for SEL**
I can describe what the term *implicit bias* means.	I can compare and contrast my implicit bias on a related topic with someone else's implicit bias on the same topic.	I can apply my knowledge and understanding of the role my own implicit bias plays in social issues, and I can recognize and empathize with those who have different perspectives.

Stage 3: Craft the driving question at the transfer level, adding authentic context for the unit.

Driving question: To what extent can we use our knowledge of the past to abolish slavery today?

Authentic context: Students will simulate what it might feel like to work for a nonprofit or philanthropic organization.

Stage 4: Create tasks that align with the success criteria (specific tasks and activities).

Surface-Level Content Tasks	Deep-Level Content Tasks	Transfer-Level Content Tasks
Reading: Read excerpts from the textbook. **Writing:** Define key terms. **Speaking:** Do a think-pair-share on key content terms.	**Reading:** Compare modern-day abolitionist writing with Civil War–era abolitionist writing. **Writing:** Use a graphic organizer to compare and contrast the economic factors of slavery in the North and South during the Civil War as well as with factors causing slavery today. **Speaking:** Conduct a class debate on the most significant economic causes of slavery.	**Reading:** Provide peer critiques on formal letters, offering different perspectives. **Writing:** Write persuasive letters that incorporate historical research. **Speaking:** Present answers to the driving question to parents, peers, and community members.

Surface-Level SEL Tasks	Deep-Level SEL Tasks	Transfer-Level SEL Tasks
Reading: Read a short article on examples of social awareness.	**Reading:** Read an article comparing and contrasting self-awareness and social awareness.	**Reading:** Read an article about connections between discrimination before the Civil War and discrimination today.
Writing: Define key terms related to social awareness, such as *empathy*, *implicit bias*, and *perspective*.	**Writing:** Write an informal journal reflection about a time when you had difficulty understanding the perspective of someone else.	**Writing:** Infuse the concept of social awareness into a persuasive letter.
Speaking: Hold a small-group discussion on what it means to be empathetic. Also, discuss the different roles and perspectives for the project (fair-trade researcher, data analysis expert, and so on).	**Speaking:** Conduct a Socratic seminar comparing and contrasting social awareness and self-awareness.	**Speaking:** Describe what society can do to be more socially aware of modern-day slavery while answering the driving question. Discuss a separate issue about which society can be more socially aware.

Stage 5: Create an entry event to launch the sustained-inquiry process.

Show a video with images and statistics of slavery in the United States during the Civil War era, as well as images and statistics of slavery from around the world today. Use a need-to-know protocol to start the inquiry process. Need-to-know categories include: (1) causes of the Civil War, (2) economic factors of slavery, (3) abolitionists and other key people, and 4) battles and military strategies.

Source: Adapted from McDowell, 2017, p. 149. Used with permission.
Source for standards: Indiana Department of Education, 2020c.

Figure 3.5: Completed example of the SPBL planning template.

*Visit **go.SolutionTree.com/21stcenturyskills** for a free blank reproducible version of this figure.*

The planning template provides a different approach than traditional PBL. As emphasized throughout this book, SPBL is focused on ensuring there is strong evidence of student learning and growth in both content knowledge and SEL skills. It places a specific emphasis on clear learning intentions and success criteria, and content knowledge and social and emotional learning have equal priority. This planning template provides an overview and vision for the sustainable PBL planning process. This five-stage process is the first step (see chapter 5, page 69) to ensure sustainability of this powerful methodology. Chapters 5–9 will depict each of the five steps for implementing sustainable PBL.

1. Plan the SPBL unit (chapter 5, page 69).

2. Develop sustainable PBL assessments (chapter 6, page 87).

3. Establish a clear goal for student learning (chapter 7, page 101).

4. Conduct teacher action research (chapter 8, page 109).

5. Reflect, refine, and celebrate the successful implementation of SPBL (chapter 9, page 121).

Moving forward in this text, we will take a close look at these five steps. Each step is important to sustaining project-based learning. In an effort to prevent what happened to Harrison School District, it is imperative that you always maintain focus on student learning. Following the five steps of SPBL and having ongoing collective inquiry around the three SPBL questions (see page 45) ensures that the product itself does not become more important than student learning.

Perspectives From the Field: Aaron Eisberg
What an Integrated-Content High School Looks Like, Sounds Like, and Feels Like

As a wall-to-wall PBL school, we want to make sure learners are continuously making connections between content and community. The power of PBL is having students connect what they are learning in the classroom and how it can be applied to current-day contexts and situations in our local community. One of our core foundational values as a school is integrating content and being able to show how content integrates across the curriculum. Our school's model centers on a collaborative culture among all teaching, leadership, and support staff roles that is designed not only out of necessity but to model what we believe is best for our students.

We are a school of four hundred students, which means we do not have a large staff. Our school is 100 percent public, 100 percent unionized, and A–G certified in the state of California. Simply put, we have the same funding formula and the same testing requirements as traditional high schools in California. Our staff for the upcoming 2021–2022 school year will be approximately fifteen teachers. So how do we ensure high-quality project-based learning within a school structure centered on the work of collaborative teams? By integrating content.

We know that in traditional environments with larger student and staff populations collaborative teams are typically structured by content-area departments. When a similar content-area department gets together, team members look through the lens of their disciplinary content. As we value multiple perspectives and multiple lenses, we structure our teams by integrated (interdisciplinary) content.

With our integrated content teams, we look at student work and continuously examine what can be done to improve student achievement. Multiple content lenses from our teachers bring different expertise levels. Each teacher brings their lens and ways to support learning and how to improve instruction and feedback. An English teacher brings grammatical expertise to a science teacher, who might bring structural and process expertise. With multiple content lenses there are also multiple opportunities for how students can apply their knowledge in different contexts. This is the power of interdisciplinary collaboration. The focus isn't just on one content area but the whole body of work and how it can be applied in different contexts.

(A. Eisberg, learning coordinator, Center for Excellence at New Tech High School, Napa, California; personal communication, December 3, 2020).

Summary

SPBL has a different approach to instruction than traditional PBL. For example, there is a specific emphasis on clear learning intentions and success criteria, and there is an equal priority placed on both content knowledge and SEL skills. The planning template in this chapter provides an overview and vision for the SPBL planning process. Completing this planning template is one of the steps in the five-step process to ensure sustainability of this powerful methodology. Moving forward in this text, you will examine each of the five steps of SPBL. Each step is essential to ensuring PBL is sustainable in your school.

Questions for Reflection

Individually or in collaborative teams, answer the following questions to reflect on your learning in this chapter.

1. In what ways do you connect with Harrison School District?

2. Of Harrison School District's three issues, which one do you think is most important? Why?

3. Which characteristics of the SPBL process are you most confident with? Why?

Challenge

Visit **go.SolutionTree.com/21stcenturyskills** to download a free blank reproducible version of figure 3.5 (page 50), and use it to begin drafting either a new or a revised SPBL unit. Start by looking at your standards and curriculum map. Determine which unit you are interested in, your learning intention, and what might be a good driving question.

CHAPTER 4

INTEGRATING SOCIAL AND
EMOTIONAL LEARNING
INTO SPBL UNITS

My brother is a pathologist. Sometimes, pathologists are referred to as a *doctor's doctor*. When a surgeon is performing surgery and comes across an unidentified tumor, for example, they call my brother. My brother then examines the tumor and determines what kind it is. He must do this in a timely fashion, and in collaboration with the surgeon.

In this scenario, my brother must answer the question *To what extent should this tumor be removed?* When faced with this challenge, my brother needs to be very specific in his response. He needs to advise the surgeon if they need to look for other tumors or if it is an isolated, benign tumor. It could be that the tumor is not yet cancerous, but it could eventually become cancerous. If my brother determines that it is cancerous, the surgeon must then alter surgical management with the patient.

There must be a very high level of trust between my brother and the surgeon. Not every patient follows a script. My brother looks at a portion of the tumor and determines a course of action. The surgeon might have more knowledge than my brother regarding the patient. The patient might have a medical history that my brother is unaware of, and at the same time, my brother has knowledge about the cells in the tumor of which the surgeon is unaware.

Both my brother and the surgeon must be aware of one another's levels of expertise. Both must also manage their emotions in this intense (at times life or death) situation and have a high level of content knowledge. However, it not only takes content knowledge to be successful in this scenario. They must also possess SEL skills.

Certainly, this scenario could result in a life or death situation for the patient. But taking a step back, I challenge you to think of a successful professional who does not need both content knowledge and SEL skills when faced with a problem. In the real world, we don't apply our content knowledge to solve a problem without also applying SEL skills. I would argue that the most effective professionals have an equal level of content knowledge and SEL skills. So, why not intentionally teach them together?

Planning and preparation are essential to SPBL units. Teachers must focus on implementing these units well. Doing things such as making adjustments based on formative assessments and milestones, answering student-generated need-to-know questions through classroom discussions, and other high-impact strategies is imperative to success. For some, a deterrent to implementing SPBL is not the concept or the philosophy but the practicality of sustaining a certain level of planning and preparation. However, an equal emphasis on content knowledge and SEL makes using the SPBL framework justifiable because in the real world, students will apply their knowledge and skills within the context of an actual problem or challenge.

A Definition of Social and Emotional Learning

A significant trend in education has been for teachers to become more intentional about growing students' social and emotional learning skills. However, many different approaches to, and definitions of, social and emotional learning exist. It is imperative that we, as educators, develop a common language around SEL. If we do not, it could lead to ambiguity and confusion, which will dilute the significance of this essential work. I chose the CASEL (n.d.a) competencies to define SEL because they have been in existence since 1994, and as a result, have been continuously refined through research. Your school or community could choose a different model, or better yet, co-define SEL with a committee of students, parents, and teachers from within your school or district.

CASEL (n.d.b) has defined five core competencies to clarify the meaning of *social and emotional learning*: (1) self-management, (2) self-awareness, (3) social awareness, (4) responsible decision making, and (5) relationship skills. These are also known as social and emotional (SEL) skills. Figure 4.1 features these five competencies, which can be taught in communities, at home, in schools, or in classrooms.

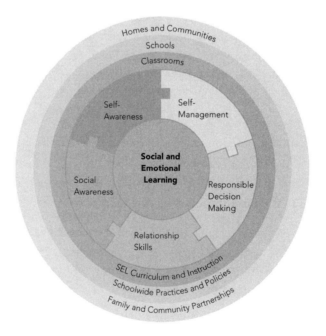

Source: CASEL, n.d.b. Used with permission.

Figure 4.1: CASEL competencies.

CASEL (n.d.b) indicates that these five competencies are teachable.

> The CASEL 5 can be taught and applied at various developmental stages from childhood to adulthood and across diverse cultural contexts. Many school districts, states, and countries have used the CASEL 5 to establish preschool to high school learning standards and competencies that articulate what students should know and be able to do for academic success, school and civic engagement, health and wellness, and fulfilling careers.

An Equal Emphasis on SEL and Academic Content

Why are SEL skills so important? According to the National Institute of Mental Health (2021), in 2019, 20.6 percent of U.S. adults (nearly one in five) suffered from some form of mental illness.

According to the American Foundation for Suicide Prevention (n.d.), in 2019:

- 47,511 Americans died from suicide.

- 1.38 million people attempted suicide.

- On average, 130 suicides occur per day.

- Suicide is the tenth leading cause of death in the United States.

- Adolescents and young adults ages fifteen to twenty-four had a suicide rate of 13.95 per 100,000.

These statistics provide some clear reasons why social and emotional learning should receive equal emphasis to academic learning in schools. Students should learn that SEL competencies are skills just like learning multiplication facts or writing skills. When teachers clearly define and teach SEL skills, students can see SEL growth just like they can see growth in learning multiplication facts.

Another *why* for increasing emphasis on SEL in schools comes from the Aspen Institute National Commission on Social, Emotional, and Academic Health, which consisted of some of the top scientists, researchers, psychologists, and educators in the United States (Jones & Kahn, 2017). The commission's report notes the importance of students' social, emotional, and academic development.

> Students who have a sense of belonging and purpose, who can work well with classmates and peers to solve problems, who can plan and set goals, and who can persevere through challenges—in addition to being literate, numerate, and versed in scientific concepts and ideas—are more likely to maximize their opportunities and reach their full potential. (Jones & Kahn, 2017, p. 4)

In other words, to maximize learning, students need to feel like they have a purpose and they belong. This has a direct connection with the PBL elements of student voice and choice and authenticity. As educators, we must try to create conditions where students feel a sense of belonging while solving problems with their peers. The report continues:

> We know that the quality and depth of student learning is enhanced when students have opportunities to interact with others and make meaningful connections to subject material. . . . Social and emotional development is multi-faceted and is integral to academics—to how school happens, and to how learning takes place. (Jones & Kahn, 2017, p. 5)

These experts went on to create statements about SEL that they all agreed on, called *consensus statements*. One of those statements says, "Social, emotional, and academic development matters" (Jones & Kahn, 2017, p. 7). Along with this consensus statement, the report notes the following:

Social, emotional, and cognitive competencies develop throughout our lives and are essential to success in our schools, workplaces, homes, and communities and allow individuals to contribute meaningfully to society.... Social, emotional, and cognitive capabilities are fundamentally intertwined—they are interdependent in their development, experience, and use.... Engaging in effective social and emotional learning-informed programs and practices can improve teacher effectiveness and well-being. (Jones & Kahn, 2017, pp. 7–8)

This group of experts agrees that these SEL skills are as important as cognitive skills; educators should want both types of skills from their ideal graduate. In other words, developing skills like responsible decision making, collaboration, and self-awareness is as important as learning about the quadratic formula or photosynthesis. Educators must consider the impact and importance of social and emotional learning for students.

The data for suicides and mental health argue that we educators have a moral obligation to address the issue of social and emotional development. It is a complicated issue, but it's one that we have the ability to address in our classrooms.

SEL and Equity

As noted previously, as educators, we have a responsibility to promote social and racial equity through culturally responsive teaching practices. Such practices lay the foundation for social and racial equity in school by promoting social and emotional learning. There are direct correlations between the five CASEL SEL competencies and culturally responsive teaching practices, as shown in figure 4.2.

CASEL Competency: Self-Awareness	Connections With Equity
• Labeling one's feelings • Relating feelings and thoughts to behavior • Accurate self-assessment of strengths and challenges • Self-efficacy • Optimism	• Examining the importance of various social identities • Deriving constructive meanings of social identities • Grounding in and affirming of cultural heritage(s)
CASEL Competency: Self-Management	**Connections With Equity**
• Regulating one's emotions • Managing stress • Self-control • Self-motivation • Stress management • Setting and achieving goals	• Coping with acculturative stress • Coping with discrimination/prejudice
CASEL Competency: Social Awareness	**Connections With Equity**
• Perspective taking • Empathy • Respect for diversity • Understanding social/ethical norms • Recognizing family, school, and community supports	• Discerning the importance of diversity (situational) • Understanding the meaning of diversity in contexts (climate) • Recognizing cultural demands and opportunities • Collective efficacy
CASEL Competency: Relationship Skills	**Connections With Equity**
• Building relationships with diverse individuals and groups • Communicating clearly • Working cooperatively • Resolving conflicts • Seeking help	• Demonstrating cultural competence • Leveraging cultural fluency

CASEL Competency: Responsible Decision Making	Connections With Equity
• Identifying problems • Analyzing situations • Solving problems • Evaluating • Reflecting • Ethical responsibility	• Considering diversity salience and climate • Assessing the impact of one's beliefs and biases • Pursuing inclusive, mutually beneficial solutions • Reflecting on broader ethical consequences of one's decisions for intragroup, intergroup, and institutional relations

Source: Jagers, Randall-Garner, & Van Ausdal, 2018, pp. 17–21.

Figure 4.2: Connections between SEL and equity.

Growing students in their understanding of themselves and their emotional intelligence helps lay the groundwork for creating more culturally aware and responsible students.

Effective SEL Integration Into Academic Curriculum

If we want students to grow in specific skills, we must first define those skills and generate a common language within classrooms and schools around those skills. For example, we might reach a consensus on the idea that students should all grow in the individual skill of collaboration, but that is an ambiguous term. What does high-quality collaboration look like, sound like, and feel like? Should you define it commonly within an entire school, or should you define collaboration differently within a course or department? If those things are outside your control, then how might you simply define collaboration within the PBL unit of study you are designing? A simple Google search for *collaboration rubrics* can provide templates, but it would be even more powerful to co-define this term with students and generate a collaboration rubric together. The idea is that you clearly define the skill and design intentional tasks and formative assessments for that skill. Clearly defining SEL skills is where using the CASEL competencies can help create a common language and clear definitions.

SEL Skills Instead of 21st Century Skills

Since I became a professional educator in 2002, a general trend has been ongoing conversations about the need to teach 21st century skills, or *soft skills*. Since the turn of the 21st century, schools have become more intentional about evaluating 21st century skills such as creativity, critical thinking, collaboration, and communication (the four Cs; Battelle for Kids, 2021).

In my experience, these four skills are among the most common responses to the question, "What are the qualities, characteristics, and dispositions we want in the ideal graduate?" However, as educators, teachers, administrators, and curriculum developers, we must streamline what we assess. The single most crucial aspect of assessing skills is defining what the skills are and ensuring that students have a clear understanding of those skills. Terms such as *collaboration* and *critical thinking* are ambiguous and challenging to quantify.

We want students to grow in both 21st century skills and social and emotional learning. However, we often do not define what we mean by these skills, and they become ambiguous. Instead of sending mixed messages about 21st century skills and social and emotional learning, we must ask, "What is the evidence for those skills? What does it look like and sound like in the classroom?" Figure 4.3 (page 60) shows a comparison of CASEL competencies and 21st century skills (or the four Cs). As you can see, the definitions of both the CASEL competencies and the four Cs consider what the evidence of learning looks like in the classroom; they become synonymous.

The CASEL Core Competencies	Evidence of Learning, or What Learning Looks Like in the Classroom	21st Century Skills
Self-awareness: • The ability to accurately recognize one's own emotions, thoughts, and values and how they influence behavior • The ability to accurately assess one's strengths and limitations, with a well-grounded sense of confidence, optimism, and a growth mindset	• Students know their personality attributes and academic strengths and weaknesses. • Students can identify where they have been, where they are, and where they are going in their learning. Students can clearly articulate learning intentions and success criteria for both academic and social and emotional learning goals. • Students know their learning gaps and can identify resources and processes to get themselves out of a learning hole.	**Creativity:** Students view failure as an opportunity to learn, and they understand that creativity and innovation are part of a long-term, cyclical process of small successes and frequent mistakes. **Critical thinking:** Students reflect critically on learning experiences and processes.
Self-management: • The ability to successfully regulate one's emotions, thoughts, and behaviors in different situations—effectively managing stress, controlling impulses, and motivating oneself • The ability to set and work toward personal and academic goals	• Students are able to set their own academic and social and emotional goals based on the specified learning intentions and success criteria for each unit of study. • Students are able to persevere through cognitive and emotional challenges with appropriate scaffolds and support. • Students are able to help construct and meet reasonable deadlines. • Students are able to identify personal motivations within the context of the learning process.	**Creativity:** Demonstrate originality and inventiveness in work and understand the real-world limits to adopting new ideas. **Critical thinking:** 1. Solve different kinds of unfamiliar problems in both conventional and innovative ways. 2. Identify and ask significant questions that clarify various points of view and lead to better solutions.
Relationship skills: • The ability to establish and maintain healthy and rewarding relationships with diverse individuals and groups • The ability to communicate clearly, listen well, cooperate with others, resist inappropriate social pressure, negotiate conflict constructively, and seek and offer help when needed	• Students are able to build trust and rapport with peers by not participating in gossip. • Students are able to give and receive appropriate constructive feedback. • Students are able to inconvenience themselves to convenience someone else. • Students are able to positively identify social capital and resources to help them achieve their goals.	**Communication:** 1. Students articulate thoughts and ideas effectively using oral, written, and nonverbal communication skills in a variety of forms and contexts. 2. Students communicate effectively in diverse environments (including multilingual and multicultural ones).

Social awareness:	
- The ability to take the perspective of and empathize with others, including those from diverse backgrounds and cultures - The ability to understand social and ethical norms for behavior and to recognize family, school, and community resources and supports	- Students self-reflect on their personal background, including aspects that have been difficult and aspects that have provided strength. - Students are able to identify and adapt their affect based on others' emotional reactions. - Students are able to genuinely put themselves in the perspective of another person. - Students are able to recognize, honor, and respect diversity.	**Collaboration:** 1. Students demonstrate the ability to work effectively and respectfully with diverse teams. 2. Students exercise flexibility and willingness to be helpful in making necessary compromises to accomplish a common goal. 3. Students assume shared responsibility for collaborative work and value the individual contributions made by each team member. **Critical thinking:** 1. Students analyze and evaluate major alternative points of view. 2. Students synthesize and make connections between information and arguments.
Responsible decision making: - The ability to make constructive choices about personal behavior and social interactions based on ethical standards, safety concerns, and social norms - The realistic evaluation of consequences of various actions and a consideration of the well-being of oneself and others	- Students are able to set and recognize smaller benchmarks in an effort to achieve the larger and ultimate goal. - Students can articulate both the positive and negative consequences of their actions. - Students can discuss how the work they produce can have a positive impact on others. - Students can both journal and think aloud to describe their goals, benchmarks to achieve those goals, and what choices it will take to ultimately accomplish those goals. - Students can be self-appraising and constructively self-critique.	**Critical thinking:** 1. Students make judgments and decisions. 2. Students solve problems. **Creativity:** 1. Students act on creative ideas to make a tangible and useful contribution to the field in which the innovation will occur. 2. Students demonstrate originality and inventiveness in work and understand the real-world limits to adopting new ideas.

Source: Adapted from CASEL, n.d.b.

Figure 4.3: Comparing CASEL competencies and 21st century skills.

*Visit **go.SolutionTree.com/21stcenturyskills** for a free reproducible version of this figure.*

In figure 4.3 (page 60), note what evidence of learning looks like for the CASEL competency of self-awareness compared to that for the 21st century skills of creativity and critical thinking. Now look at the CASEL competency of self-management. Comparing self-management with creativity and critical thinking, and viewing the comparison through the lens of what evidence of learning looks like in the classroom, you can see the shared connections. These connections include students setting their own goals based on clear learning intentions and success criteria, and persevering through cognitive and emotional challenges (with appropriate scaffolds and support). Observe the connections for the CASEL competencies of relationship skills, social awareness, and responsible decision making as well.

We know from Hattie's research that providing students with feedback has a high effect size (0.92) on student learning (Visible Learning Meta^X, n.d.). One way to provide students with feedback is through assessment. One might argue that feedback and assessment are synonymous.

SEL Skills for Assessment

In a well-designed and well-implemented SPBL unit, students will grow in many skills; however, choose one specific SEL skill, ensure that it is clear, and be intentional about giving feedback on that skill throughout the process. Providing ongoing feedback throughout makes the PBL process much more practical and meaningful for students. Providing students with ongoing feedback regarding their SEL growth is one of the distinguishable differences between traditional PBL and SPBL. Just like a pathologist applies both knowledge and SEL skills to a given a problem, you should ask the same of students and provide the support they need to complete assignments successfully. As educators, we must integrate SEL skill development with content knowledge development, because this is what professionals do in the real world.

Figure 4.4 shows an example of an eighth-grade social studies curriculum map. Note that it includes an equal commitment to identifying a content learning intention and an SEL learning intention for each unit. The SEL learning intention should have a direct connection with the content learning intention. The SPBL framework allows you to effectively integrate both an SEL skill and the elements of PBL, or at least some of the elements of PBL (in this case, a driving question, authenticity, and sustained inquiry), as an instructional framework. One can see that some of the driving questions go straight to the heart of not only the content learning intention but also the SEL learning intention. You cannot provide meaningful feedback on learning unless the intention of learning is clear. Adding an SEL learning intention for each unit of study is a way to clearly define and provide intentional feedback on the desired skills for students.

Overview for the Year: Eighth-Grade Social Studies

Unit of Study or Curriculum Context	Research Analysis	Colonization and Revolution	Constitution	Westward Expansion and Industrial Revolution	Civil War	Reconstruction (Rebuilding Richmond, Virginia, After the Civil War)	Voice and Choice Essay
Content Learning Intention	I can produce and present a personal narrative.	I can apply my understanding of the concept of liberty and the American Revolution to a modern-day situation.	Based on my knowledge of the U.S. Constitution, I can formulate an opinion on the role government should play in moral decisions.	I can apply knowledge of the U.S. westward expansion from historical research.	I can apply the knowledge I gain from historical research on the causes of the U.S. Civil War to create connections and solutions.	I can evaluate the challenges and benefits of individuals' and societies' inalienable rights.	I can reflect on the content knowledge and skills I have gained this year and produce an essay on a topic that is important to me.
CASEL SEL Skill	Introduction to all SEL skills	Self-awareness	Self-management	Responsible decision making	Social awareness	Relationship skills	Reflection on growth in all SEL skills
SEL Learning Intention	I can reflect on the five CASEL competencies for myself.	I can apply my own strengths and perceptions.	I can set my own goals, manage my impulses, and meet deadlines.	I can evaluate my individual role in the ethics of a variety of contexts.	I can present the perspective of another race on an issue of discrimination.	I can evaluate the individual role I have within a high-functioning team.	I can self-evaluate my growth in the five CASEL competencies.
Driving Question	How do we know what we know?	Where should we create liberty today?	When should the government play a role in moral decisions?	Why is there a cost to progress?	To what extent can we use our knowledge of the past to abolish slavery today?	Who is responsible for creating a community that truly offers life, liberty, and the pursuit of happiness?	The driving question is based on individual interests.
Duration	Two weeks	Six weeks	Six weeks	Six weeks	Six weeks	Six weeks	Three weeks
Culminating Event or Performance Product	Presentation in front of parents sharing yearly goals	Presentation to representatives from the Red Cross and parents to generate awareness of Haitian orphans	Presentation to lawyers, professors, doctors, or lobbyists	Presentation to business professionals or CEOs, Native Americans, Hoosier Environmental Council members, or environmental scientists	Presentation to representatives from organizations such as World Vision or Amnesty International	Rebuilding Richmond presentation to city council members, architects, or ACLU members	Presentation to an authentic audience depending on students' essay topics.
Simulated Profession (Authentic Context)	Counselor or psychologist	Investigative journalist or web designer	Lawyer or attorney	CEO or sales representative who works in competitive global markets	A professional from a nonprofit or philanthropic organization such as Amnesty International or World Vision	City planner, architect, surveyor, or engineer	Not applicable

Figure 4.4: Example SPBL curriculum map.

As previously discussed, effectively integrating a connected SEL skill into your PBL unit ensures that there is equal emphasis on the SEL skill and the content. These simultaneous learning outcomes justify PBL as a sustainable and comprehensive instructional framework. This framework prevents SEL from being set aside as a separate activity or something that is done *in addition to* the curriculum.

Perspectives From the Field: Kyle Miller
A Districtwide Approach to Social and Emotional Learning

The renowned American psychologist B. F. Skinner said, "Education is what survives when what has been learned has been forgotten" (Skinner, 1964). Our educational institutions are bursting with academic standards and standardized tests developed to measure the content we want students to know. However, when you ask a student, "What is your favorite subject?" or "Who is your favorite teacher?" the response you hear typically has little to do with the subject matter. Yes, education is about building knowledge, but an equally important task is to nurture the essential social and emotional skills students need to navigate the global society they will find themselves in postgraduation. The abilities to think critically, collaborate effectively with others, and manage the complexities of relationships are the essential educational remnants that must endure when the memory of important dates, events, and formulas fades. We have search engines for content, but we need sustaining social and emotional skills to successfully navigate life.

In Westfield Washington Schools, we view learning as an interdependent social, emotional, and cognitive process. In fact, many of the areas of the brain that process emotion, cognition, and language are all intertwined (Jones & Kahn, 2017). Therefore, in order for learning to occur, it is imperative to develop instructional systems that engage all domains of learning—social, emotional, and academic—in an integrated environment. Social and emotional learning does not happen in a vacuum, only at designated times of day or solely through a specific program or curriculum. Instead of purchasing a curriculum and calling it good, we have worked hard to cultivate four simple, but far from simplistic, conditions for comprehensive districtwide social and emotional learning implementation.

Condition 1: Cultivate District Leadership

You may have heard people say, "It starts with the adults." In order for social and emotional learning initiatives to take hold, it's essential to spend time learning by doing. In the initial stages of SEL implementation, we allocated intentional time in district administration meetings to build our own social and emotional awareness, knowledge, and skill prior to discussing programs or curricula. Our district administration team explored the nine types of enneagrams (or personality types) to build individual and collective awareness of the lens through which we see the world (The Enneagram Institute®, 2021). This helped lay the foundation for how we interact with one another, build community, and navigate difficult situations and conversations (the very same skills we want to teach our students). In addition, each of our buildings spent time exploring a variety of tools to develop self-awareness and build a deeper understanding of those around them. We believe that SEL is not something we do *to* our students: it's something we do *with* our students.

Condition 2: Establish Common Knowledge, Beliefs, and Practices

As our district administrative team and building-level personnel deepened their knowledge and self-awareness, it was important to begin developing a shared vision. We used documents from the Aspen Institute's National Commission on Social, Emotional, and Academic Development to build an understanding of the research supporting learning as an interdependent process (*How Learning Happens* [2017] and *From a Nation at Risk to a Nation at Hope* [2018]). Utilizing these documents, we co-created our district belief statements of social and emotional learning to ground our work and practice.

Using this knowledge, and guided by the belief that SEL happens in an integrated environment, we began to develop consistent practices throughout the district to build social, emotional, and academic competence (for example, morning meetings, engaging and collaborative instructional practices, mindful moments, brain breaks, calm corners, co-created classroom and building expectations, hallway greetings). We provided professional development opportunities focused on helping staff understand the impact of adverse childhood experiences, educational neuroscience, diversity, equity, inclusion, and restorative practices on classroom instruction and intervention. We believe that all staff members bear the responsibility of building SEL competencies in students.

Condition 3: Build Leadership Capacity Within Schools

Successful implementation hinges on building teacher leaders and developing collective efficacy. A crucial step for systemic change is the creation of building-level SEL teams. Building-level teams and teacher leadership provide the infrastructure necessary to explore building-level student data, develop building-level strategic plan goals, and help support buy-in from staff. We believe all teachers are leaders, and we must be intentional about building their skills and providing opportunities for them to lead their peers.

Condition 4: Evaluate Systems and Processes to Carry Out and Sustain SEL Implementation

One characteristic of an effective educator is the ability to reflect and reimagine the ways in which school happens. For sustainable SEL implementation to occur, a district must continually reevaluate the systems and processes in place to more effectively serve staff and students. Time is always the most valuable commodity, and like most districts, we didn't feel like we had enough time for all the professional development necessary. Therefore, we collaborated with our district administrators, community, and school board to implement a late start for students one day a week to provide weekly opportunities for staff development. We also reimagined staff and administrative meetings to provide a designated time for collective inquiry and professional development. We reimagined the role of team and department leaders to shift away from the nuts-and-bolts facilitator to an organized structure of collaborative teams with leaders integrating PLC content. The roles and structures have always existed; we believe that if you change the way you look at things, the things you look at will change.

There are multiple ways to achieve districtwide comprehensive implementation of social, emotional, and academic development. The four conditions previously described provide a framework for considering the essential elements needed to successfully navigate implementation

continued ▶

of SEL skills. Ask yourself, "How will we cultivate district leadership? How will we establish common knowledge, beliefs, and practices that fit our student population? How will we build teacher leadership capacity, and how might we look at our systems and processes to reimagine how school happens?"

(K. Miller, coordinator of social and emotional learning, Westfield Washington Schools, Westfield, Indiana; personal communication, January 18, 2021)

Summary

Some of the skills we, as educators, want the ideal graduate to attain include collaboration, critical thinking, problem solving, communication, and creativity. We also want them to have a high aptitude in SEL skills such as responsible decision making, social awareness, self-awareness, self-management, and relationship skills. We should think about 21st century skills and SEL skills as synonymous. Consider the evidence of learning for these skills. They also are synonymous. If we craft learning intentions in our units of study around the CASEL SEL competencies, students will grow in 21st century skills as well. Social and emotional learning and academic learning should be integrated and emphasized with equal intensity.

Questions for Reflection

Individually or in collaborative teams, answer the following questions to reflect on your learning in this chapter.

1. In what ways are 21st century skills (the four Cs) and social and emotional learning (CASEL competencies) synonymous?

2. How do you feel about the idea of teaching the CASEL SEL competencies with as much intensity as academic standards?

3. In which of the five SEL competencies (self-awareness, social awareness, responsible decision making, relationship skills, and self-management) are you strongest? Which ones are more of a challenge? What about your students—where do they have strengths and challenges?

Challenge

Review the curriculum map in figure 4.4 (page 63) and your own units of study or curriculum map. Determine one SEL competency that might align with one of your units of study.

PART II

THE *HOW* OF SUSTAINABLE PROJECT-BASED LEARNING

CHAPTER 5

STEP 1: PLANNING THE SPBL UNIT

The first part of this book was about the *what* and *why* of PBL. We also explored some of the pitfalls and gaps in PBL. We saw this both in John Hattie's (2009) research and also more anecdotally through the hypothetical Harrison School District case study (page 39). PBL takes a long time to plan, and if not designed correctly, might not result in effective student learning.

Part II is the heart of the book. This is where theory is put into a clear, step-by-step design and implementation process. In this part, I will continue to use the eighth-grade social studies unit example as the anchor unit, the Modern-Day Abolitionist. Each of the five steps has planning template examples. These templates are meant to make the SPBL process clear, practical, and most important, focused on student learning. As we work through these steps, the SPBL process was created to ensure that although the PBL elements are extremely important, the evidence of student learning should always be the ultimate goal.

The way we ensure that the focus remains on evidence of student learning is to focus on the three SPBL questions. As we begin to go through the five-step SPBL process, keep these three questions in mind.

1. How do you ensure at least one year's growth in one year's time?

2. How do you ensure an equal intensity of surface-, deep-, and transfer-level learning for each unit of study?

3. How do you define and provide intentional feedback to students on their growth in both content knowledge and SEL skills?

These three questions go to the heart of the *why* for SPBL. When you stop focusing on these three questions, that is often when the sustainability part of the process starts to waiver.

As noted previously, the SPBL process has five steps.

1. Plan the SPBL unit.

2. Develop sustainable PBL assessments.

3. Establish a clear goal for student learning

4. Conduct teacher action research.

5. Reflect, refine, and celebrate the successful implementation of SPBL.

This chapter focuses on step 1—Plan the SPBL unit.

The Five Stages for Planning an SPBL Unit

Planning a sustainable PBL unit includes five stages. Those stages, based on McDowell's (2017) steps to planning a rigorous PBL unit, are as follows.

Stage 1: Create a learning intention for both academic content and SEL.

Stage 2: Develop content and SEL success criteria for each level of learning (surface, deep, and transfer).

Stage 3: Craft the driving question at the transfer level, adding authentic context for the unit.

Stage 4: Create tasks that align with the success criteria.

Stage 5: Create an entry event to launch the sustained-inquiry process.

Create a Learning Intention for Both Academic Content and SEL

Learning intentions, brief statements that describe what the student should know and be able to do (McDowell, 2017), are major concepts from the content that justify an entire unit of study (for example, historical research, the quadratic equation, and persuasive writing). Learning intentions are void of context. The learning intention should drive the context; the context should not drive the learning intention. (You might want to eventually create an SPBL curriculum map with an academic content and SEL learning intention for each unit throughout the year, as shown in figure 4.4, page 63.) Figure 5.1 shows example learning intentions for eighth-grade social studies. Note that the learning intentions in this figure are written at the transfer level and void of any specific context or product. The SEL learning intention should hold equal importance to the content learning intention.

Stage 1: Create a learning intention for both academic content and SEL (a major concept for the unit and a CASEL competency).

1. Content learning intention: I can apply the knowledge I gain from historical research on the causes of the U.S. Civil War to create connections and solutions (8.1.11, 8.1.20, 8.1.21, 8.1.22, 8.1.23, 8.1.24, 8.1.25, 8.4.2, 8.4.3, LH.1, LH.2, LH.3, LH.4, LH.5, LH.6, LH.7).

2. SEL learning intention (social awareness): I can present the perspective of another race on an issue of discrimination.

Source for standards: Indiana Department of Education, 2020c.

Figure 5.1: Example of academic and SEL learning intentions.

Figure 5.2 is a checklist for creating learning intentions. As you develop your learning intentions, you may use this checklist as a reflection tool. (See figure 9.1, page 123, for a full list of checklists.)

Checklist for Creating Learning Intentions
Learning intentions: ☐ Are written in clear, student-friendly language (*I can . . . , I will . . .*) ☐ Are written at the transfer level (application) ☐ Allow the context to be applied to another context ☐ Clearly connect content and social and emotional learning

Figure 5.2: Checklist for creating learning intentions.

*Visit **go.SolutionTree.com/21stcenturyskills** for a free reproducible version of this figure.*

Develop Content and SEL Success Criteria for Each Level of Learning (Surface, Deep, and Transfer)

Now that you have created the learning intention, you should generate the success criteria at each level of learning (surface, deep, and transfer). Success criteria are specific learning targets that state what students must demonstrate at the surface, deep, and transfer levels to meet the learning intention (McDowell, 2017). The process of crafting the success criteria is where clarity becomes paramount. Success criteria are the language you want students to use during the learning process. Figure 5.3 provides sentence stems for each learning level. These sentence stems will help you develop success criteria.

Sentence Stems for Surface-Level Success Criteria	Sentence Stems for Deep-Level Success Criteria	Sentence Stems for Transfer-Level Success Criteria
• I can define . . . • I can describe . . . • I can name . . .	• I can analyze the meaning of . . . • I can compare and contrast . . . • I can determine the cause and effect of . . .	• I can apply _____ in a new or different context. • I can apply what I learned in this class to another class . . . • I can hypothesize about . . . • Based on my knowledge and understanding, I will design . . .

Figure 5.3: Sentence stems for learning-level success criteria.

Figure 5.4 is a checklist for creating effective success criteria. You can use this checklist as you plan the success criteria for your unit.

Checklist for Developing Success Criteria
Success criteria: ☐ Provide the ingredients to meet the learning intention ☐ Focus on learning at each level (surface, deep, and transfer) rather than tasks or activities ☐ Can be articulated by students ☐ Align to exemplars and models that address quality ☐ Allow students some level of ownership in crafting them

Figure 5.4: Checklist for developing success criteria.

*Visit **go.SolutionTree.com/21stcenturyskills** for a free reproducible version of this figure.*

Once you craft the content learning intention and success criteria, use the same checklists and processes for crafting an SEL learning intention and success criteria. I recommend starting with the academic learning intention and then determining which of the five CASEL competencies connect best with it. Once you determine the competency, you can develop the SEL learning intention. When creating learning intentions, envision what student exemplar products, presentations, or writing samples might look like or sound like that go to the heart of the learning intention. Once students have a clear vision of what exemplar evidence of learning looks, sounds, and feels like, ask them, "What makes this learning artifact successful?" Have students generate a list, and use this list, written in student-friendly language, for your success criteria.

Figure 5.5 shows a completed example of stage 1 and stage 2 of the SPBL planning template, including clear learning intentions and success criteria for both content and the designated SEL skill (social awareness).

SPBL Planning Template		
Stage 1: Create a learning intention for both academic content and SEL (a major concept for the unit and a CASEL competency).		
1. Content learning intention: I can apply the knowledge I gain from historical research on the causes of the U.S. Civil War to create connections and solutions (8.1.11, 8.1.20, 8.1.21, 8.1.22, 8.1.23, 8.1.24, 8.1.25, 8.4.2, 8.4.3, LH.1, LH.2, LH.3, LH.4, LH.5, LH.6, LH.7). **2. SEL learning intention (social awareness):** I can present the perspective of another race on an issue of discrimination.		
Stage 2: Develop content and SEL success criteria for each level of learning (daily learning goals). *You could have multiple goals, written without context or specificity.*		
Surface-Level Success Criteria for Content I can define key terms such as *abolitionist, yeoman, popular sovereignty, limited* or *total war,* and so on.	**Deep-Level Success Criteria for Content** I can compare and contrast the economic causes of slavery in the pre–Civil War era with the economic causes of slavery today.	**Transfer-Level Success Criteria for Content** I can apply my knowledge and understanding of the past and solve a problem that exists today (answer to the driving question).
Surface-Level Success Criteria for SEL I can describe what the term *implicit bias* means.	**Deep-Level Success Criteria for SEL** I can compare and contrast my implicit bias on a related topic with someone else's implicit bias on the same topic.	**Transfer-Level Success Criteria for SEL** I can apply my knowledge and understanding of the role my own implicit bias plays in social issues, and I can recognize and empathize with those who have different perspectives.

Source: Adapted from McDowell, 2017. Used with permission.
Source for standards: Indiana Department of Education, 2020c.

Figure 5.5: Learning intentions and success criteria.

Remember, when you think about success criteria, you might think of it as creating daily and weekly learning targets. Ideally, the language in the success criteria is what you want your classroom to sound like. If learning intentions are the cake, success criteria are the eggs, milk, and sugar. Depending on the duration of your unit of study, you should have multiple examples of success criteria for each level of complexity. There is no magic number; refer to your learning intention to help guide you and the number of standards that students are going to learn throughout the process.

Craft the Driving Question at the Transfer Level, Adding Authentic Context for the Unit

PBL is an attractive instructional framework because the individual units of study begin with a driving question or challenge that starts at the transfer level. Remember, transfer learning is when students can apply their content knowledge and skills in a new or different context. This new or different context should be authentic—some sort of real-world context so students see how the content applies in the world outside of school. Posing a driving question or challenge from the beginning helps students understand why the content they are learning matters.

If the learning intention is written at the transfer level, use this to help craft your driving question. For our example, looking at the sample unit on the U.S. Civil War, the driving question might be, *To what extent can we use our knowledge of the past to abolish slavery today?* The learning intention involves historical research. At the end of this unit, we want students to know about historical research and to realize that the ultimate learning goal was about historical research. Upon completion, we want students to say that the project was about historical research, *not* that the project was about slavery. Slavery is the context, not the content.

As noted previously, stages 1 and 2 involve creating learning intentions and success criteria that are void of context. You will add context when you craft the driving question. Too often in PBL, students get caught up in the context of the project instead of the learning. Let's look at the driving question for the anchor unit as an example. It is written at the transfer level:

To what extent can we use our knowledge of the past to abolish slavery today?

If the learning intention is historical research, the context is the issue of modern-day slavery. Next year, the context might change to something different. Following are some examples of different contexts you could use for the same learning intention.

- Create awareness about our local community's role in the Civil War.

- Create awareness of modern-day abolitionist movements. Determine the advantages of certain military strategies used in the U.S. Civil War that might apply to other wars.

Once you create the learning intentions, success criteria, and driving question for one unit, consider doing it for multiple units. Figure 5.6 (page 74) is an example of a yearlong curriculum map of the overarching curriculum context—learning intentions, SEL skills, and driving questions. This map helps you see how those features are clearly aligned and integrated.

Curriculum Context	Research Analysis	Colonization and Revolution	Constitution	Westward Expansion and Industrial Revolution	Civil War	Reconstruction	Voice and Choice Essay
Content Learning Intention	I can produce and present a personal narrative.	I can apply my understanding of the concept of liberty and the American Revolution to a modern-day situation.	Based on my knowledge of the U.S. Constitution, I can formulate an opinion on the role government should play in moral decisions.	I can apply knowledge of the U.S. westward expansion through historical research.	I can apply the knowledge I gain from historical research on the causes of the U.S. Civil War to create connections and solutions.	I can evaluate the challenges and benefits of societies' inalienable rights.	I can reflect on the content knowledge and skills I have gained this year and produce an essay on a topic that is important to me.
CASEL SEL Skill	Introduction to all SEL skills	Self-awareness	Self-management	Responsible decision making	Social awareness	Relationship skills	Reflection on growth in all SEL skills
SEL Learning Intention	I can reflect on the five CASEL competencies for myself.	I can apply my own strengths and perceptions.	I can set my own goals, manage my impulses, and meet deadlines.	I can evaluate my individual role in the ethics of a variety of contexts.	I can present the perspective of another race on an issue of discrimination.	I can evaluate the individual role I have within a high-functioning team.	I can self-evaluate my growth in the five CASEL competencies.
Driving Question	How do we know what we know?	Where should we create liberty today?	When should the government play a role in moral decisions?	Why is there a cost to progress?	To what extent can we use our knowledge of the past to abolish slavery today?	Who is responsible for creating a community that truly offers life, liberty, and the pursuit of happiness?	The driving question is based on individual interests.

Figure 5.6: Examples of content learning intentions, SEL learning intentions, and driving questions.

Each driving question is grounded in the learning intention. If you have a transfer-level learning intention and clear success criteria at each level—surface, deep, and transfer—then you can change the context from year to year, which allows for more options. Consider the following examples.

- Where should we create liberty . . .

  - In our school?

  - In our community?

  - In our personal lives?

- When should the government play a role in . .

  - Immigration law?

  - Free speech?

  - Personal health?

- Why is there a cost to . . .

  - Social migration?

  - Specific types of economic systems such as capitalism?

  - Manifest destiny?

A challenge with PBL is that a teacher might take hours and hours to plan a PBL unit that has relevant context, and then the next year, that context is no longer relevant. All of a sudden, the unit is no longer usable. To stick with the anchor unit example, there might come a day (hopefully) when modern-day slavery is no longer an issue. If that day comes, the context of the unit will change, but the learning intention (core standard of historical research) will not. You can easily prevent that if you follow these three stages.

1. Create a learning intention for both academic content and SEL.

2. Develop content and SEL success criteria for each level of learning (surface, deep, and transfer).

3. Craft the driving question at the transfer level, adding authentic context for the unit.

Figure 5.7 is a checklist for crafting the driving question. You may use this checklist as a tool for reflection as you develop your SPBL unit.

Checklist for Crafting the Driving Question
The driving question:
☐ Restates the learning intention as a question
☐ Is written at the transfer level (*To what extent . . . , When . . . , Who . . . , Where . . .*)
☐ Provides the "Why does this matter?" (authenticity)
☐ Adds context

Figure 5.7: Checklist for crafting the driving question.

*Visit **go.SolutionTree.com/21stcenturyskills** for a free reproducible version of this figure.*

Figure 5.8 shows the addition of the authentic context to crank up the authenticity of the unit. Note that the unit focus is on learning, not the product or context.

Stage 1: Create a learning intention for both academic content and SEL (a major concept for the unit and a CASEL competency).		
1. Content learning intention: I can apply the knowledge I gain from historical research on the causes of the U.S. Civil War to create connections and solutions (8.1.11, 8.1.20, 8.1.21, 8.1.22, 8.1.23, 8.1.24, 8.1.25, 8.4.2, 8.4.3, LH.1, LH.2, LH.3, LH.4, LH.5, LH.6, LH.7). **2. SEL learning intention (social awareness):** I can present the perspective of another race on an issue of discrimination.		
Stage 2: Develop content and SEL success criteria for each level of learning (daily learning goals). *You could have multiple goals, written without context or specificity.*		
Surface-Level Success Criteria for Content I can define key terms such as *abolitionist, yeoman, popular sovereignty, limited or total war,* and so on.	**Deep-Level Success Criteria for Content** I can compare and contrast the economic causes of slavery in the pre–Civil War era with the economic causes of slavery today.	**Transfer-Level Success Criteria for Content** I can apply my knowledge and understanding of the past and solve a problem that exists today (answer to the driving question).
Surface-Level Success Criteria for SEL I can describe what the term *implicit bias* means.	**Deep-Level Success Criteria for SEL** I can compare and contrast my implicit bias on a related topic with someone else's implicit bias on the same topic.	**Transfer-Level Success Criteria for SEL** I can apply my knowledge and understanding of the role my own implicit bias plays in social issues, and I can recognize and empathize with those who have different perspectives.
Stage 3: Craft the driving question at the transfer level, adding authentic context for the unit.		
Driving question: To what extent can we use our knowledge of the past to abolish slavery today? **Authentic context:** Students will simulate what it might feel like to work for a nonprofit or philanthropic organization.		

Source for standards: Indiana Department of Education, 2020c.

Figure 5.8: Example of PBL unit plan, stages 1–3.

Create Tasks That Align With the Success Criteria

Some might argue that entire units of study or complete yearlong courses should be spent learning at the surface level. SPBL instead emphasizes that students need to understand the application of content within each unit of study. There should be "equal intensity and integration of surface, deep, and transfer learning" (McDowell, 2021, p. 4), and I would add that this definition of rigor could apply for each individual unit of study. In order to achieve this rigor, one must intentionally design a unit with tasks at each of the three learning levels—surface, deep, and transfer. Furthermore, SPBL places equal value on SEL skills and content knowledge, so you need to develop tasks to accomplish all of these aspects.

Figure 5.9 shows some examples of surface-, deep-, and transfer-level learning tasks.

Surface-Level Tasks *Build knowledge.*	Deep-Level Tasks *Make meaning and connections.*	Transfer-Level Tasks *Apply understanding.*
• Take notes on a lecture. • Learn vocabulary. • Work through basic mathematics problems. • Recite and recall facts. • Memorize. • Identify key terms or facts. • Label items. • Match items.	• Determine cause and effect. • Compare and contrast. • Write something in your own words. • Make inferences.	• Answer a transfer-level driving question with concrete evidence and support. • Apply a concept in a new and different situation. • Justify a response to the driving question using a different context or perspective.

Source: Adapted from McDowell, 2017, p. 45. Used with permission.

Figure 5.9: Examples of tasks for each learning level.

It is important to be mindful about which tasks are appropriate for each level of learning. Figure 5.10 shows an example of a surface-level task in which students must define key terms related to the learning intention and driving question.

Term	Picture or Visual (Draw a visual depiction of the term.)	Definition in Your Own Words
Emancipation Proclamation		
Contrabands		
Habeas corpus		
Copperhead		
Total war		
Anaconda Plan		

Figure 5.10: Example of a surface-level task.

Figure 5.11 shows an example of a deep-level task in which students compare and contrast the North and South in the pre–Civil War era with the United States today. It might seem tempting to use this as an example of a transfer-level task. However, when implemented in the classroom, it is just about students' ability to compare and contrast, not their ability to apply understanding.

	North Before the Civil War	South Before the Civil War	United States Today
Key Exports and Businesses			
Way of Life and Infrastructure			
Political Views			
View of Slavery			
Key People			

Figure 5.11: Example of a deep-level task.

Figure 5.12 shows an example of a transfer-level task in which students might answer the driving question. Note the last example, where students are using their knowledge of historical research and applying it in a different context (immigration rather than modern-day slavery). This would be an example of students transferring their knowledge and skill of historical research from one context to another.

Driving Question:	Proficient
To what extent can we use our knowledge of the past to abolish slavery today?	• I can apply writing strategies from past abolitionists to my own writing. • I can cite multiple texts and connect them to a formulated personal opinion with key steps to abolish modern-day slavery. • I can explain how I applied the process of historical research step by step to address a problem other than modern-day slavery (such as the modern-day immigration dilemma).

Figure 5.12: Example of a transfer-level task.

Developing intentional tasks is essential in the SPBL planning process. Figure 5.13 is a checklist for creating appropriate-leveled tasks.

Checklist for Creating Tasks
Tasks: ☐ Ensure students show evidence of learning at each level of complexity (surface, deep, and transfer)   ☐ Include reading, writing, and speaking at each level of complexity   ☐ Embed Hattie's high-impact strategies (Visible Learning Meta[X], n.d.; see figure 1.4, page 14).

Figure 5.13: Checklist for creating tasks.

Visit **go.SolutionTree.com/21stcenturyskills** *for a free reproducible version of this figure.*

Figure 5.14 shows stage 4 of the anchor unit planning template (Modern-Day Slavery).

Stage 4: Create tasks that align with the success criteria (specific tasks and activities).		
Surface-Level Content Tasks **Reading:** Read excerpts from the textbook. **Writing:** Define key terms. **Speaking:** Do a think-pair-share on key content terms.	**Deep-Level Content Tasks** **Reading:** Compare modern-day abolitionist writing with Civil War–era abolitionist writing. **Writing:** Use a graphic organizer to compare and contrast the economic factors of slavery in the North and South during the Civil War with economic factors today. **Speaking:** Conduct a class debate on the most significant economic causes of slavery.	**Transfer-Level Content Tasks** **Reading:** Provide peer critiques on formal letters, offering different perspectives. **Writing:** Write persuasive letters that incorporate historical research. **Speaking:** Present answers to the driving question to parents, peers, and community members.
Surface-Level SEL Tasks **Reading:** Read a short article on examples of social awareness. **Writing:** Define key terms related to social awareness, such as *empathy*, *implicit bias*, and *perspective*. **Speaking:** Hold a small-group discussion on what it means to be empathetic. Also, discuss the different roles and perspectives for the project (fair-trade researcher, data analysis expert, and so on).	**Deep-Level SEL Tasks** **Reading:** Read an article comparing and contrasting self-awareness and social awareness. **Writing:** Write an informal journal reflection about a time when you had difficulty understanding the perspective of someone else. **Speaking:** Conduct a Socratic seminar comparing and contrasting social awareness and self-awareness.	**Transfer-Level SEL Tasks** **Reading:** Read an article about connections between discrimination before the Civil War and discrimination today. **Writing:** Infuse the concept of social awareness into the persuasive letter. **Speaking:** Describe what society can do to be more socially aware of modern-day slavery while answering the driving question. Discuss a separate issue about which society can be more socially aware.

Figure 5.14: Example of PBL unit plan, stage 4.

Create an Entry Event to Launch the Sustained-Inquiry Process

The entry event is the fifth and final stage in planning an SPBL unit. Review figure 2.8 (page 30), which shows an example of an entry document. The entry document is part of the entry event. The entry event is essential for sustaining PBL for two reasons. First, it shows students the *why* of the unit and the application of the learning. This is what starts students at the transfer level; the entry event depicts the application of the learning intention right from the beginning. Second, it launches the sustained-inquiry process. The entry event is a feature that separates SPBL from traditional teaching, because from the very beginning, students see the real-world application of their learning, or the transfer. Traditional teaching typically starts with surface-level learning and then eventually builds into transfer (as shown in figure 1.4, page 14).

You can format the entry event in a variety of ways. Following are a few ideas for entry events.

- Video-conference with an outside expert who is attempting to answer a similar driving question.

- Use a controversial article.

- Facilitate a lively discussion.

- Generate a puzzling problem.

- Present startling statistics.

- Show an inspiring or emotional video clip.

- Invite a guest speaker into the classroom.

Figure 5.15 provides a checklist for creating an entry event.

Checklist for Creating an Entry Event
The entry event:
☐ Ensures student-generated need-to-know questions go to the heart of both the academic and SEL learning intentions
☐ Is embedded with the driving question
☐ Ensures students are clear about what learning transfer looks and sounds like
☐ Makes it so students are able to answer the question, "Why are we learning this?"

Figure 5.15: Checklist for creating an entry event.

*Visit **go.SolutionTree.com/21stcenturyskills** for a free reproducible version of this figure.*

Note how the completed SPBL planning template in figure 5.16 meets the success criteria for all five stages. There is an equal balance of SEL and academics throughout the entire planning process.

Stage 1: Create a learning intention for both academic content and SEL (a major concept for the unit and a CASEL competency).

1. Content learning intention: I can apply the knowledge I gain from historical research on the causes of the U.S. Civil War to create connections and solutions (8.1.11, 8.1.20, 8.1.21, 8.1.22, 8.1.23, 8.1.24, 8.1.25, 8.4.2, 8.4.3, LH.1, LH.2, LH.3, LH.4, LH.5, LH.6, LH.7).

2. SEL learning intention (social awareness): I can present the perspective of another race on an issue of discrimination.

Stage 2: Develop content and SEL success criteria for each level of learning (daily learning goals).

You could have multiple goals, written without context or specificity.

Surface-Level Success Criteria for Content	**Deep-Level Success Criteria for Content**	**Transfer-Level Success Criteria for Content**
I can define key terms such as *abolitionist, yeoman, popular sovereignty, limited or total war,* and so on.	I can compare and contrast the economic causes of slavery in the pre–Civil War era with the economic causes of slavery today.	I can apply my knowledge and understanding of the past and solve a problem that exists today (answer to the driving question).
Surface-Level Success Criteria for SEL	**Deep-Level Success Criteria for SEL**	**Transfer-Level Success Criteria for SEL**
I can describe what the term *implicit bias* means.	I can compare and contrast my implicit bias on a related topic with someone else's implicit bias on the same topic.	I can apply my knowledge and understanding of the role my own implicit bias plays in social issues, and I can recognize and empathize with those who have different perspectives.

Stage 3: Craft the driving question at the transfer level, adding authentic context for the unit.

Driving question: To what extent can we use our knowledge of the past to abolish slavery today?

Authentic context: Students will simulate what it might feel like to work for a nonprofit or philanthropic organization.

Stage 4: Create tasks that align with the success criteria (specific tasks and activities).

Surface-Level Content Tasks	**Deep-Level Content Tasks**	**Transfer-Level Content Tasks**
Reading: Read excerpts from the textbook. **Writing:** Define key terms. **Speaking:** Do a think-pair-share on key content terms.	**Reading:** Compare modern-day abolitionist writing with Civil War–era abolitionist writing. **Writing:** Use a graphic organizer to compare and contrast the economic factors of slavery in the North and South during the Civil War with economic factors today. **Speaking:** Conduct a class debate on the most significant economic causes of slavery.	**Reading:** Provide peer critiques on formal letters, offering different perspectives. **Writing:** Write persuasive letters that incorporate historical research. **Speaking:** Present answers to the driving question to parents, peers, and community members.

Figure 5.16: Completed example of the SPBL planning template.

continued ▶

Stage 4: Create tasks that align with the success criteria (specific tasks and activities).		
Surface-Level SEL Tasks	**Deep-Level SEL Tasks**	**Transfer-Level SEL Tasks**
Reading: Read a short article on examples of social awareness. **Writing:** Define key terms related to social awareness, such as *empathy*, *implicit bias*, and *perspective*. **Speaking:** Hold a small-group discussion on what it means to be empathetic. Also, discuss the different roles and perspectives for the project (fair-trade researcher, data analysis expert, and so on).	**Reading:** Read an article comparing and contrasting self-awareness and social awareness. **Writing:** Write an informal journal reflection about a time when you had difficulty understanding the perspective of someone else. **Speaking:** Conduct a Socratic seminar comparing and contrasting social awareness and self-awareness.	**Reading:** Read an article about connections between discrimination before the Civil War and discrimination today. **Writing:** Infuse the concept of social awareness into the persuasive letter. **Speaking:** Describe what society can do to be more socially aware of modern-day slavery while answering the driving question. Discuss a separate issue about which society can be more socially aware.

Stage 5: Create an entry event to launch the sustained-inquiry process.
Show a video with images and statistics of slavery in the United States during the Civil War era, as well as images and statistics of slavery today. Use a need-to-know protocol to start the inquiry process. Need-to-know categories include (1) key people involved, (2) economic factors of slavery, (3) abolitionists and other key people, and (4) battles and military strategies.

Source: Adapted from McDowell, 2017. Used with permission.
Source for standards: Indiana Department of Education, 2020c.

Once you have planned the learning intentions, success criteria, driving question, tasks, and entry event, and the learning is clearly the priority, use the seven PBL design elements to guide you throughout implementation of the unit.

To begin implementation, you might want to create an SPBL curriculum map (refer to figure 4.4, page 63, to see a completed SPBL curriculum map). There are pros and cons to creating an initial SPBL curriculum map. By creating this map, you might feel overwhelmed at first or think that you must do wall-to-wall SPBL (meaning you only implement SPBL units all year). However, the advantages of creating a map include the following.

- You can determine which SEL skill fits best with which content topic.

- You can determine in which unit of study you want to implement all seven elements of PBL (could be one, could be all).

- You can determine a direction for the year and begin to craft a vision for what one year's growth in one year's time might be.

- You can provide a variety of authentic contexts for students.

- You can ensure that the content is more important than the context.

Figure 5.17 shows a complete overview of the five stages and checklists for creating an SPBL unit.

Checklists for Planning an SPBL Unit	
Stages	**Checklists**
Stage 1: Create a learning intention for both academic content and SEL.	Learning intentions: ☐ Are written in clear, student friendly language (*I can . . . , I will . . .*) ☐ Are written at the transfer level (application) ☐ Allow the context to be applied to another context ☐ Clearly connect content and social and emotional learning
Stage 2: Develop content and SEL success criteria for each level of learning (surface, deep, and transfer).	Success criteria: ☐ Provide the ingredients to meet the learning intention ☐ Focus on learning at each level (surface, deep, transfer) rather than tasks or activities ☐ Can be articulated by students ☐ Align to exemplars and models that address quality ☐ Allow students to have some level of ownership in crafting them
Stage 3: Craft the driving question at the transfer level, adding authentic context for the unit.	The driving question: ☐ Restates the learning intention as a question ☐ Is written at the transfer level (*To what extent . . . , When . . . , Who . . . , Where . . .*) ☐ Provides the "Why does this matter?" (authenticity) ☐ Adds context
Stage 4: Create tasks that align with the success criteria.	Tasks: ☐ Ensure students show evidence of learning at each level of complexity (surface, deep, and transfer) ☐ Include reading, writing, and speaking at each level of complexity ☐ Embed Hattie's high-impact strategies
Stage 5: Create an entry event to launch the sustained-inquiry process.	The entry event: ☐ Ensures student-generated need-to-know questions go to the heart of both the academic and SEL learning intentions ☐ Is embedded with the driving question ☐ Ensures students are clear about what learning transfer looks and sounds like ☐ Makes it so students are able to answer the question, "Why are we learning this?"

Figure 5.17: Checklists for planning an SPBL unit.

*Visit **go.SolutionTree.com/21stcenturyskills** for a free reproducible version of this figure.*

Tips for Planning an SPBL Unit

Following are some helpful tips for implementing the five stages of SPBL for a unit of study.

- **Answer critical questions:** As you plan your unit, the ultimate goal is to address the following SPBL questions (CASEL, n.d.b).

    a. How do you ensure at least one year's growth in one year's time?

    b. How do you ensure an equal intensity of surface-, deep-, and transfer-level learning for each unit of study?

    c. How do you define and provide intentional feedback to students on their growth in both content knowledge and SEL skills?

- **Always start with your state or provincial standards:** Learning intentions must be grounded in standards. Pull out the major themes and concepts as you develop your units and learning intentions.

- **Write learning intentions at the transfer level (application, evaluation):** Remember that learning intentions are brief statements that describe what students should know and be able to do. They are significant concepts from the content that justify an entire unit of study (for example, historical research, the quadratic equation, and persuasive writing).

  Remember success criteria are specific learning targets that state what students must demonstrate at the surface, deep, and transfer levels to meet the learning intention (McDowell, 2017). Often, learning intentions are daily or weekly learning targets. Think of the learning intention as the cake and the success criteria as the ingredients. Consider presenting students with the learning intention and then co-constructing the success criteria with them.

- **Write a driving questions at the transfer level:** Consider starting your driving question with a sentence stem such as *To what extent . . . , When . . . , Who . . . ,* or *Where. . . .*

- **Create a list of all the strategies and tasks you or your team implement individually and collectively in the classroom:** The strategies and tasks should be completely void of context. For example, if you use a vocabulary strategy for a specific unit, keep the process you use; just change the vocabulary words for each unit. Once you create the list, sort the strategies into three categories: (1) surface, (2) deep, and (3) transfer. Now, you have a list of tasks that you can insert in the SPBL planning template.

- **When determining the PBL elements equalizer, you do not need to implement the same number of PBL elements for each unit:** This tip holds true as long as there is a conscious effort to implement all the elements to some degree. For example, if you want to crank down the voice and choice for a particular unit, that's OK. The goal is an equal intensity of surface, deep, and transfer levels of learning. However, you should challenge yourself to incorporate at least one unit during the year that intentionally includes all seven elements.

- **Determine authentic context for your units:** To help achieve this, ask yourself or your team, "How are the standards applied in the real world? Who applies them? In what context are they applied?"

- **Use the PBL equalizer to reflect on your use of the seven PBL design elements before, during, and after implementation of the unit:** Although the seven elements should never override student learning, they are an excellent vehicle to promote learning, so be mindful of the level of student voice and choice, authenticity, reflection, critique and revision, sustained inquiry, and the quality of the driving question and culminating public product.

Summary

There are five stages to planning a sustainable PBL unit: (1) create a learning intention for both academic content and SEL; (2) develop content and SEL success criteria for each level of learning (surface, deep, and transfer); (3) craft the driving question at the transfer level, adding authentic context for the unit; (4) create tasks that align with the success criteria; and (5) create an entry event to launch the sustained-inquiry process.

Teachers implementing PBL might be deterred by the fact that planning a SPBL unit takes longer than more traditional methods. However, if you create a bank of tasks at each level of complexity (surface, deep, and transfer), you can simply change the *context* of the tasks instead of the *process* of the tasks, which will save time when planning future units. PBL should be about the learning intention, not the context of the learning. Again, once you approach it this way, you can recycle tasks and just change the context from unit to unit.

Questions for Reflection

Individually or in collaborative teams, answer the following questions to reflect on your learning in this chapter.

1. Why should you write learning intentions at the transfer level?

2. How will you make connections between the content learning intention and the SEL learning intention within your unit of study?

3. What are some examples of surface-, deep-, and transfer-level tasks for both your SEL success criteria and your academic success criteria?

4. What are some ideas for an authentic context for your unit?

Challenge

Use the SPBL template with the SPBL checklists to design a new unit or revise an old unit you have implemented.

CHAPTER 6

STEP 2: DEVELOPING
SPBL ASSESSMENTS

After returning from a long road trip, you might find that the stops along the way were as meaningful or perhaps even more meaningful than the final destination. When you think about SPBL, the formative assessments along the way are certainly as meaningful, if not more so, than the final product. Although the final product can be amazing, it's the learning throughout the process that allows for feedback and growth.

Just like some of your favorite vacations, SPBL is a journey. However, instead of an amusement park or a balmy tropical island, your ultimate destination is student learning, which results in the qualities and characteristics of the ideal graduate. In order to ensure this journey is a successful one, you must have strong assessments and feedback strategically placed along the way.

This chapter explores how to provide students feedback in their growth in both SEL skills and academic content through the creation of common assessments using four essential assessment documents: (1) an SPBL culminating public product rubric, (2) a summative assessment for surface and deep learning, (3) a formative assessment calendar, and (4) an anticipated need-to-know map.

Common Assessments

Creating common assessments allows you to have meaningful dialogue with colleagues about evidence of learning. There is additional benefit to developing common assessments, as it can enhance collective teacher efficacy. According to Hattie's research, collective teacher efficacy has an effect size of 1.36 (Visible Learning Meta[X], n.d.). Collective teacher efficacy has proven to lead to over three years' growth in one year's time. Visible Learning Plus (as cited in Waack, 2018) defines collective teacher efficacy as:

> The collective belief of the staff of the school/faculty in their ability to positively affect students. [Collective teacher efficacy] has been found to be strongly, positively correlated with student achievement. A school staff that believes it can collectively accomplish great things is vital for the health of a school and if they believe they can make a positive difference then they very likely will.

Teachers can improve their collective efficacy by having meaningful conversations with colleagues around growth in student learning based on common SPBL assessments. In an ideal scenario, teachers would have designated collaboration time to co-plan SPBL units and establish common assessments based on agreed-on learning intentions and success criteria. (I discuss this in more detail in chapter 7, page 101.)

Sustainable PBL is a process in which teachers provide intentional feedback to students on their growth in SEL and academic skills and content. In the ideal scenario, teachers work in collaborative teams. It is possible to implement SPBL individually, but it is more effective if teacher teams develop common assessments. In high schools and middle schools, many educators teach just one subject area (such as electives), which makes it difficult to develop common assessments. In these circumstances, singletons can collaborate with other teachers within their department or who have somewhat similar courses.

You might not be able to develop common assessments, but you will be able to conduct step 4 of the SPBL process—*Conduct teacher action research.* You can work with each other on developing surface, deep, and transfer tasks and discuss evidence of learning. You can also gather feedback from each other when creating assessments and determining surface-, deep-, and transfer-level questions. So even if you do not have the ability to develop a true common assessment, you can still have a meaningful SPBL experience.

The Four Essential Documents for SPBL Assessment

As you begin planning assessments for your SPBL unit, you need to create the following four essential documents: (1) SPBL culminating public product rubric, (2) summative assessment for surface and deep learning, (3) anticipated need-to-know map, and (4) formative assessment calendar. Creating these documents requires a thorough understanding of how to use assessments within the SPBL process. The purpose of these assessment documents is to ensure you stay focused on the three SPBL questions.

1. How do you ensure at least one year's growth in one year's time?

2. How do you ensure an equal intensity of surface-, deep-, and transfer-level learning for each unit of study?

3. How do you define and provide intentional feedback to students on their growth in both content knowledge and SEL skills?

Keeping those questions in mind, SPBL promotes the use of both quantitative and qualitative forms of assessment to measure growth and provide practical feedback to students. Cornell University (n.d.b) defines *quantitative assessment* as "data collection that assigns numbers to objects, events, or observations according to some rule." In contrast, Cornell University (n.d.a) defines *qualitative assessment* as "analysis used to tell a story or demonstrate key themes" and "detailed descriptions of people, events, situations, interaction, and observed behaviors." In the SPBL model, you will use more qualitative measurements to assess growth in the SEL learning intention and more quantitative measurements to assess growth in the content learning intention, specifically for surface and deep levels of knowledge. In addition, it is imperative in this model to use the language of the three levels (surface, deep, and transfer) when developing and implementing assessments to effectively measure both growth in content and SEL skills.

Table 6.1 describes the *what* and *why* for each of these four essential documents.

TABLE 6.1: The *What* and *Why* of the Four Essential Documents for SPBL Assessment

Assessment Document	The *What*	The *Why*
SPBL Culminating Public Product Rubric	It has the same and consistent success criteria based on the learning intention from the SPBL unit planner. This helps ensure clarity, consistency, and practicality. There is a strong effort to ensure students demonstrate an equal intensity of all three levels of learning. The focus is more on the evidence of learning than the product.	It reemphasizes the learning intentions and success criteria. It provides clarity for both the students and the teacher regarding the vision for the learning process. It provides clarity for key formative assessments or milestones throughout the process. It is the final destination for the unit and helps answer the three SPBL questions.
Summative Assessment for Surface and Deep Learning	There is a pre- and postassessment to measure student growth in surface and deep learning. It is based on the determined surface- and deep-level success criteria from the SPBL unit planner.	It provides clarity for key surface- and deep-level formative assessments. It allows students and the teacher to prepare for mandated standardized tests. It ensures students are learning the content learning intention and content at the necessary level.
Anticipated Need-to-Know Map	It includes key milestones that allow for evidence of student learning at all three levels (surface, deep, and transfer), planning backward from the culminating public product. When designing the unit, the teacher generates the ideal need-to-knows they want students to ask at each level (surface, deep, and transfer) before each milestone (or phase of the unit). If the anticipated need-to-knows surpass your expectations, adjust instruction accordingly. If the need-to-knows do not meet your expectations, adjust instruction accordingly (for example, implement some direct instruction).	It helps promote critical thinking within the sustained-inquiry process. Student-generated need-to-knows are a key formative assessment that helps the teacher gauge where students are in their learning based on the need-to-knows they create throughout the unit. If student need-to-knows are not aligning with teacher-anticipated need-to-knows, it is time to make teaching adjustments.
Formative Assessment Calendar	It is like a traditional unit calendar planned backward from the culminating public product. It includes intentional surface, deep, and transfer assessments that are both quantitative (lead up to the summative assessment for surface and deep learning) and qualitative (lead up to the culminating public product rubric for transfer learning, often in the form of key milestones building up to the product). Note: Use a variety of ways to implement formative assessments throughout the unit.	It crafts a clear vision for the ideal growth track for both the SEL and content learning intentions.

*Visit **go.SolutionTree.com/21stcenturyskills** for a free reproducible version of this table.*

The following sections detail the four essential documents for SPBL assessments.

SPBL Culminating Public Product Rubric

When planning your SPBL unit assessment, begin with the end in mind. This helps create a clear vision for what you want students' work to look like and sound like when it comes to applying their learning. The first assessment document to create is the SPBL culminating public product rubric. The culminating public product should do the following.

- Provide an opportunity for students to demonstrate their knowledge of all three levels of learning (surface, deep, and transfer).

- Provide an opportunity for students to answer the driving question.

- Showcase the authenticity of students' experiences.

- Demonstrate high-quality craftsmanship, defined as students having multiple opportunities to revise their work.

Figure 6.1 shows an example rubric for an SPBL unit's culminating public product. This rubric is an example of a summative assessment. The culminating public product is summative. In this chapter, you will learn how to provide meaningful feedback to students throughout the SPBL process. You will also see how formative feedback throughout the SPBL unit is more important than the feedback at the end. However, the common rubric provides a clear destination for where you want students to be at the end of the unit. You can create this rubric once you have established your success criteria. Note that the success criteria in figure 6.1 have been copied directly from the SPBL planning template in figure 5.16 (page 81).

Driving Question: To what extent can we use our knowledge of the past to abolish slavery today?				
Learning Intentions	**4 Exemplary** Clear evidence of equal intensity of all three learning levels (surface, deep, and transfer)	**3 Proficient** Transfer-level learning (Apply understanding in a different context.)	**2 Progressing** Deep-level learning (Make meaning.)	**1 Not Yet** Surface-level learning (Build knowledge.)
Content learning intention: I can apply the knowledge I gain from historical research on the causes of the U.S. Civil War to create connections and solutions.	• I can apply my knowledge and understanding of the past and solve a problem that exists today (answer to the driving question). • I can compare and contrast the economic causes of slavery in the pre–Civil War era with the economic causes of slavery today. • I can define key terms such as *abolitionist, yeoman, popular sovereignty, limited* or *total war,* and so on.	I can apply my knowledge and understanding of the past and solve a problem that exists today (answer to the driving question).	I can compare and contrast the economic causes of slavery in the pre–Civil War era with the economic causes of slavery today.	I can define key terms such as *abolitionist, yeoman, popular sovereignty, limited* or *total war,* and so on.

SEL learning intention (social awareness): I can present the perspective of another race on an issue of discrimination.	• I can apply my knowledge and understanding of the role my own implicit bias plays in social issues, and I can recognize and empathize with those who have different perspectives. • I can compare and contrast my implicit bias on a related topic with someone else's implicit bias on the same topic. • I can describe what the term *implicit bias* means.	I can apply my knowledge and understanding of the role my own implicit bias plays in social issues, and I can recognize and empathize with those who have different perspectives.	I can compare and contrast my implicit bias on a related topic with someone else's implicit bias on the same topic.	I can describe what the term *implicit bias* means.
Evidence of High-Quality Work	**2 Exemplary**	**1 Not Yet**		
Craftsmanship	• There is evidence of care and precision in the final product. • There is evidence of multiple drafts or rehearsals. • There is evidence of revision based on constructive feedback from others.	Not all exemplary criteria have been met.		
Authenticity	• The work uses formats and standards from the professional world. • The work contributes to a larger context or community. • The work has been created for a public audience beyond the classroom. • There is evidence of the student's personal voice.	Not all exemplary criteria have been met.		

Figure 6.1: Example SPBL culminating public product rubric.

This rubric provides clarity around the destination measurement for the culminating public product and the transfer of student learning. Ideally, students should be able to identify the success criteria at each level; this helps them become capable of self-assessment. You should always want students to be able to answer these three questions.

1. Where am I in my learning?

2. Where have I been in my learning?

3. Where am I going in my learning?

Figure 6.2 provides a checklist for the SPBL culminating public product rubric. Use this as a reflection tool when crafting the culminating public product rubric for your unit. As you plan your assessments throughout the unit, starting with this rubric will help you create a vision for what you want students to be able to do and know at the end of the unit.

Assessment Document	Checklist
SPBL Culminating Public Product Rubric	☐ It has the same and consistent success criteria based on the learning intention from the SPBL unit planner. This helps ensure clarity, consistency, practicality. ☐ There is a strong effort to ensure students demonstrate an equal intensity of all three levels of learning. ☐ The focus is more on the evidence of learning than the product.

Figure 6.2: Checklist for SPBL culminating public product rubric.

*Visit **go.SolutionTree.com/21stcenturyskills** for a free reproducible version of this figure.*

Summative Assessment for Surface and Deep Learning

SPBL units will typically have two summative assessments. One would might look like a traditional assessment (multiple choice, matching, short answer, and so on) that gauges students' surface and deep learning. For upper-level courses, such as an AP course, this is where you might provide students with AP sample test questions. These would be examples of quantitative measurements of growth.

Prior to implementing the unit of study with students, you must have a common quantitative assessment that can measure growth in surface- and deep-level success criteria. As stated previously, surface-level knowledge includes understanding key vocabulary and key facts. Deep level knowledge would determine students understanding of cause and effect and their ability to compare and contrast. Planning the pre- and postassessments is essential, as they help address the question, "How do you ensure at least one year's growth in one year's time?" Having a preassessment and postassessment helps you determine where students were when they began the unit and where they are when the unit has ended. As a result, you can measure the growth in their learning.

Quantitative summative assessments within the context of an SPBL unit include traditional assessments that have standardized test–like questions (for example, multiple-choice, short-answer, and essay questions). Typically, these assessments ensure students are learning at the surface and deep levels. At the high school level, you can use examples of AP, International Baccalaureate, or state or provincial standardized test questions to help with development. The SPBL process emphasizes that students should perform well on public products and performances *and* regular standardized tests.

Figure 6.3 provides an example of a common summative assessment you might use to gather quantitative data for an SPBL unit. Note that the questions are meant to assess student learning at the surface and deep levels.

Deep (analyze)

1. Most Northerners opposed the Fugitive Slave Act because it:

  a. Endangered their way of life since a large number of fugitive slaves lived in the North.

  b. Encouraged slaves to resort to rebellion and violence to protest the new law.

  c. Gave commissioners too much power and should have allowed slaves the right to a jury trial.

  d. Ended the progress that the antislavery movement had made in the South.

Surface (recall)

2. The First Battle of Bull Run:

  a. Shattered the Union's hope of winning the war quickly and easily.

  b. Showed the Union that the Confederate army was weaker than anticipated.

  c. Demonstrated to the Confederacy the power and strength of the Union army.

  d. Destroyed the Confederacy's hope of restoring unity without resorting to war.

Deep (explain)

3. Which statement best expresses the reason why the Southern states decided to secede from the Union after the election of 1860?

  a. The Southern economy and way of life would be destroyed.

  b. Slaves would begin an uprising if the states did not secede.

  c. Seceding from the Union would end the possibility of war.

  d. Secession would end the conflicts between Northern states over slavery.

Deep (explain)

4. Why did President Lincoln wait until after the Union victory at the Battle of Antietam to announce the Emancipation Proclamation?

  a. He thought the North would support his decision after the victory.

  b. He wanted to catch the Confederacy off guard.

  c. He wanted the Union to be in a position of strength.

  d. He thought the South would be more receptive to the Proclamation at that time.

Surface (recall)

5. What did the 15th Amendment say?

Surface (define)

6. What was a carpetbagger?

Deep (explain)

7. If the North had so many advantages when the war began (more people, manufacturing, supplies), why did the war last so long?

Figure 6.3: Example common quantitative questions from a summative assessment measuring surface and deep learning.

In the SPBL process, an assessment like this is essential for several reasons, such as the following.

- It assesses students on their surface and deep levels of learning.
- It is similar to what students might find on standardized tests.
- It provides an opportunity for preassessment.
- It provides an opportunity for the development of common quantitative formative assessments.

In summary, SPBL quantitative assessments are beneficial because they measure student growth at the surface and deep levels. Figure 6.4 offers a checklist for creating a summative assessment for surface and deep learning. You can use this checklist as a reflection tool when planning your summative assessments.

Assessment Document	Checklist
Summative Assessment for Surface and Deep Learning	☐ There is both a pre- and postassessment to measure student growth in their surface and deep levels of learning. ☐ The assessment is based on the determined surface- and deep- level success criteria from the SPBL unit planner.

Figure 6.4: Checklist for summative assessment for surface and deep learning.

*Visit **go.SolutionTree.com/21stcenturyskills** for a free reproducible version of this figure.*

Anticipated Need-to-Know Map

The next planning document within the SPBL assessment process is the anticipated need-to-know map. This map is important because (1) it helps hold students accountable for the sustained-inquiry process, and (2) it helps teachers determine whether their anticipated need-to-knows align with students' need-to-knows. Figure 6.5 is an example anticipated need-to-know map.

Anticipated Need-to-Know Map

Milestone 1	Milestone 2	Milestone 3	Milestone 4	Milestone 5	Milestone 6
Entry event video: *To what extent can we use our knowledge of the past to abolish slavery today?*	Key vocabulary chart	Compare-and-contrast chart comparing slavery before the U.S. Civil War with slavery today	Tuning Protocol: initial exhibit design that incorporates key vocabulary terms and visuals comparing economic factors of the North and South, to economic factors in the 21st century that create unfair labor practices.	Formal writing assignment: text analysis of an excerpt from the writing of an abolitionist, such as: • Harriet Beecher Stowe • William Lloyd Garrison • Abraham Lincoln	Final museum exhibit
Anticipated Surface-Level Need-to-Knows	**Anticipated Surface- and Deep-Level Need-to-Knows**	**Anticipated Surface- and Deep-Level Need-to-Knows**	**Anticipated Deep- and Transfer-Level Need-to-Knows**	**Anticipated Transfer-Level Need-to-Knows**	**Anticipated Transfer-Level Need-to-Knows**

• What does *abolish* mean?
• What is an abolitionist?
	• Why did the South think slavery was OK?
	• Who is an abolitionist today?
		• How can we use visuals and data to generate awareness of the issues in our exhibit?	• What peer feedback will we apply to our products?
			• How did abolitionists of the past write so persuasively?
				• To what extent do our products answer the driving question?	• In what situation should a perspective different than mine be applied to the answer of the driving question?
					• To what extent can we use our knowledge of the past to do the following?
					  – Eliminate discrimination
					  – Promote social justice
					  – Prevent war

Figure 6.5: Example anticipated need-to-know map.

As you plan your anticipated need-to-know map, you can use figure 6.6 as a checklist for reflection.

Assessment Document	Checklist
Anticipated Need-to-Know Map	☐ It includes key milestones that allow for evidence of student learning at all three levels (surface, deep, and transfer), planning backward from the culminating public product.
	☐ When designing the unit, generate the ideal need-to-knows you want students to ask at each level (surface, deep, and transfer) before each milestone (or phase of the unit). If students' anticipated need-to-knows surpass your expectations, adjust instruction accordingly. If the need-to-knows do not meet your expectations, adjust instruction accordingly (for example, implement some direct instruction).

Figure 6.6: Checklist for anticipated need-to-know map.

Visit go.SolutionTree.com/21stcenturyskills for a free reproducible version of this figure.

Formative Assessment Calendar

The final assessment document is similar to what you might use as a unit calendar. The difference is, it is a unit calendar created within the context of the design of an SPBL unit. The focus is solely on formative assessments and milestones that will be the evidence of growth and learning at each of the three levels (surface, deep, and transfer).

The formative assessment calendar will help you visualize when to implement a formative assessment when a milestone is due. Think of milestones as *essential tasks*; they serve as key formative assessments throughout the unit and as significant benchmarks to monitor student understanding and progress.

A *milestone* is a major event, building block, or formative assessment within the context of an SPBL unit of study. Milestones are essential in the SPBL process to check for understanding as well as help drive the sustained-inquiry process. Milestones should progress from surface to deep to transfer levels of learning. For example, if a culminating public product is a student presentation on findings from a research paper, one of the first milestones would be a list of sources they are going to use. The next milestone might be an outline, and another milestone would be a first draft. These are key building blocks leading up to the culminating public product. Since milestones are typically stepping stones that ultimately lead to the culminating public product, they help tell the story, and are qualitative measurements of growth at each of the three levels of learning.

Formative assessments are *for* learning, a formal or an informal check for student understanding that teachers can use to alter or adjust their instruction.

In *Embedded Formative Assessment*, Dylan Wiliam (2017) describes the five strategies for effective formative assessments.

1. Clarifying, understanding, and sharing learning intentions

2. Engineering effective classroom discussions, tasks, and activities that elicit evidence of learning

3. Providing feedback that moves learners forward

4. Activating students as learning resources for one another

5. Activating students as owners of their own learning

These five strategies should all be prevalent within the context of the formative assessment calendar and the implementation of the items within the formative assessment calendar for your SPBL unit. Now, put these strategies in the context of the three levels of learning.

- **Surface-level formative assessments:** Milestones or tasks in which students demonstrate building knowledge, such as defining key vocabulary terms or displaying knowledge of basic facts

- **Deep-level formative assessments:** Milestones or tasks in which students demonstrate making meaning or developing connections, such as comparing and contrasting, establishing cause and effect, or being able to answer *why*

- **Transfer-level formative assessments:** Milestones or tasks in which students demonstrate applying knowledge in a new or different context, such as answering the driving question from a different role or perspective

Figure 6.7 shows an example of a completed formative assessment map. Note that there is an intentional effort to balance formative assessments to promote an equal intensity of surface, deep, and transfer learning. In addition, there is a balance between quantitative and qualitative assessments, all striving to provide students with feedback on their growth in both content knowledge and SEL skills.

Day	Type of Assessment	Week 1 (Causes of the Civil War)	Week 2 (Economic Factors)	Week 3 (Abolitionists)	Week 4 (Military Strategy)	Week 5
Monday	Quantitative					
	Qualitative	Need-to-knows (NTKs) from the entry event	Review NTKs from the entry event and new NTKs.	Review NTKs from the entry event and new NTKs.	Peer edit on formal writing assignment draft (Deep)	
Tuesday	Quantitative	Two multiple-choice questions for warm-up activity (Surface)		Two multiple-choice questions for warm-up activity (Surface and deep)		Summative assessment made up of multiple-choice and short-answer questions (Surface and deep)
	Qualitative		Create a compare-and-contrast chart comparing slavery during the Civil War era with slavery today. (Deep)	Create a metaphor or analogy comparing free trade versus fair trade in the 21st century. (Deep and transfer)	Describe what society can do to be more socially aware of modern-day slavery while answering the driving question. State a separate issue where society can be more socially aware. (SEL) (Transfer)	

Wednesday	Quantitative	Vocab check (Surface)		Socratic seminar comparing and contrasting the difference between social awareness and self-awareness (Deep)		
	Qualitative		Informal journal reflection about a time when you had difficulty understanding the perspective of someone else (SEL) (Deep)		Review NTKs from the entry event and new NTKs. (Surface, deep, and transfer)	.
Thursday	Quantitative	Five multiple-choice questions for warm-up activity (Surface)				
	Qualitative			Tuning Protocol on initial exhibit design, switching (Deep)	Formal writing assignment due. (Transfer)	
Friday	Quantitative	Vocabulary quiz and eight-question multiple-choice quiz on cause of the U.S. Civil War (Surface)	Seven-question multiple-choice quiz on the economic factors surrounding the U.S. Civil War (Surface and deep)	Eight-question multiple-choice quiz on key people and abolitionists (Surface and deep)	Ten-question multiple-choice quiz on military strategy (Surface and deep)	
	Qualitative					Culminating public product: interactive museum exhibit Culminating public product rubric (Transfer)

Figure 6.7: Example SPBL formative assessment calendar.

Figure 6.8 (page 98) is a checklist you can use for reflection and guidance while creating your SPBL formative assessment calendar.

Assessment Document	Checklist
Formative Assessment Calendar	☐ It is like a traditional unit calendar planned backward from the culminating public product. ☐ It includes intentional surface, deep, and transfer assessments that are both quantitative (lead up to the summative assessment for surface and deep learning) and qualitative (lead up to the culminating public product rubric for transfer learning, often in the form of key milestones building up to the product).

Figure 6.8: Checklist for formative assessment calendar.

Visit **go.SolutionTree.com/21stcenturyskills** for a free reproducible version of this figure.

Effective Assessment of Growth in SEL Skills

There are different ways you can quantify SEL skills and measure growth in those skills. When assessing student growth, decide if you want a qualitative or quantitative approach. Some organizations work to quantify SEL skills, motivation skills, or personality skills. The Enneagram Institute® (www.enneagraminstitute.com), LionsLead (www.lionslead.com), Indigo (www.indigoproject.org/asu-online), and Panorama (www.panoramaed.com/surveys) all provide excellent assessments that identify aspects of social and emotional learning, personality traits, and motivations. Typically, these organizations follow a specific process for assessment. Students take an assessment at the beginning of the first year they are in the school (for example, sixth grade in middle school or freshman year in high school). The baseline assessment through the form of a survey determines a baseline. Students then receive a report that clearly defines their skills, which teachers have access to, and they retake the survey several times throughout their time in that school. The students can observe their growth via the reports' clear definitions of skills. Taking a quantitative approach can be effective, but qualitative assessment is also an effective method in SPBL.

Just as students need to be capable of self-assessing their content learning intentions so they can state where they are, where they have been, and where they are going, they should be able to do the same for their SEL learning intentions. You can approach assessing SEL skills the same way you approach content knowledge. Just as you have clear content standards, learning intentions, and success criteria and tasks for content at each level of learning, you must have the same for identified SEL skills, which you have already intentionally designed (see chapter 5, page 69). Just as you might show students an exemplary piece of writing, you should show students exemplary modeling of SEL skills. Half the battle with assessing SEL skills is to clearly define them for students.

Use the final culminating public product rubric (see figure 6.1, page 90) you created as the vision for an SEL exemplar. Two simple strategies to model SEL skills at an exemplary level include the following.

1. Show a video clip and have students evaluate the example using the SEL success criteria. For example, if you chose the SEL skill of self-awareness and defined it for students, show students examples of what a self-aware person might sound like. Perhaps it's a video clip of a self-reflection or a monologue depicting the skill.

2. Implement the Fishbowl Protocol shown in figure 6.9. A key aspect of the Fishbowl Protocol is that students are explicitly clear on the SEL learning intention and success criteria. Students develop their assessment capabilities by evaluating a group of their peers in looking for surface-, deep-, and transfer-level evidence of the SEL learning intention.

Fishbowl Protocol

Framing	Determine a pair or team that is demonstrating a skill at an exemplary level (based on the rubric).				Four minutes
Rubric Study	Provide the class with the rubric or at least a clear depiction of the learning intention and success criteria for the skill.				
	Driving Question: To what extent can we use our knowledge of the past to abolish slavery today?				
	4 Exemplary Clear evidence of equal intensity of all three learning levels (surface, deep, and transfer)	**3 Proficient** Transfer-level learning (Apply understanding in a different context.)	**2 Progressing** Deep-level learning (Make meaning.)	**1 Not Yet** Surface-level learning (Build knowledge.)	
	SEL learning intention (social awareness): I can present the perspective of another race on an issue of discrimination.	I can apply my knowledge and understanding of the role my own implicit bias plays in social issues, and I can recognize and empathize with those who have different perspectives. I can compare and contrast my implicit bias on a related topic with someone else's implicit bias on the same topic. I can describe what the term *implicit bias* means.	I can apply my knowledge and understanding of the role my own implicit bias plays in social issues, and I can recognize and empathize with those who have different perspectives.	I can compare and contrast my implicit bias on a related topic with someone else's implicit bias on the same topic.	I can describe what the term *implicit bias* means.
Inside Circle and Outside Huddle	Have the chosen pair or team model a conversation or whatever you observed the students doing that demonstrated the skill. Put those students in the center of the room. They should carry on the conversation or model the skill as if no one else were watching. Simultaneously, have the rest of the class take notes and critique the pair or team based on the rubric. Use sentence stems, such as *I noticed that . . .* or *I have a question about. . . .*				Ten minutes
Reflection	Encourage an open dialogue between the inside group (students who were observed) and the outside group (students who were taking notes and recording feedback).				Five minutes
Total time:					Nineteen minutes

Source: Adapted from EL Education, 2017, p. 17.

Figure 6.9: Fishbowl Protocol.

Tips for Developing SPBL Assessments

Following are some helpful tips for developing SPBL assessments.

- Use the SPBL planning template (figure 5.16, page 81) to create your SPBL culminating public product rubric (see figure 6.1, page 90, as an example).

- Once you have gone through the SPBL planning process and feel comfortable creating success criteria, consider exemplars and co-construct your success criteria and SPBL culminating public product rubric with students.

- Plan backward for both the traditional written assessment (assessing surface- and deep-level learning) and the culminating public product (assessing surface-, deep-, and transfer-level learning).

- Ideally, students should use the language of the success criteria throughout the SPBL unit. This helps them to be assessment-capable learners.

- SEL skills are important, and you must ensure that students have clarity on what those skills look, sound, and feel like. Be intentional about modeling the application of these skills.

Summary

When designing the assessments for an SPBL unit, the intent is to provide students with feedback in their growth in both content and SEL skills. There are four key documents you should create to help in the SPBL assessment process: (1) an SPBL culminating public product rubric, (2) a summative assessment for surface and deep learning, (3) an anticipated need-to-know map, and (4) a formative assessment calendar. In addition to creating these planning documents, be sure to design specific tasks for SEL skills at each level of learning just as you would the tasks for content knowledge.

Questions for Reflection

Individually or in collaborative teams, answer the following questions to reflect on your learning in this chapter.

1. When developing the SPBL culminating public product rubric, what did the conversation sound like between you and your colleagues when you discussed evidence of student learning at the surface, deep, and transfer level for both SEL and content learning intentions?

2. Out of the four assessment documents, which one is most similar to an assessment process you currently follow? Which one is most different? Why?

3. As you reflect on your completed formative assessment map, is there an equal intensity of surface, deep, and transfer formative assessments distributed throughout the unit?

Challenge

Use the Fishbowl Protocol to model a specific skill in class this week (see figure 6.9, page 99, for an example).

CHAPTER 7

STEP 3: ESTABLISHING A CLEAR GOAL FOR STUDENT LEARNING

Throughout the book, I have emphasized that what makes PBL sustainable is to have a foundation in the pedagogy, but ensuring that there is clear evidence of student learning throughout the unit is also vital. You can debate pedagogy, but it is difficult to debate positive and clear evidence of student learning at all three levels. In chapter 6 (page 87), you designed your SPBL assessments. Once you have planned your SPBL unit and your assessments, it is time to craft a goal for student learning. This chapter discusses how to establish a clear goal around student learning for your SPBL unit.

Let's begin by creating a SMART goal. First I will discuss the *how* for creating SMART goals. Next, I will discuss the *why*, including the benefits of creating goals in collaboration with colleagues. I will address the differences between and the value of using qualitative and quantitative measurements for growth within the context of your SPBL unit. Finally, this chapter emphasizes why using protocols to engage in conversations around student learning data is an integral part of crafting your learning goal.

SMART Goals

Crafting a SMART (strategic and specific, measurable, attainable, results oriented, and time bound) goal on the established learning intentions gives you an opportunity to estimate student achievement and also helps you determine both student growth and achievement (Conzemius & O'Neill, 2014). The format of a SMART goal includes the following.

- **Strategic and specific:** The goal is direct and detailed. The example in figure 7.1 (page 103) shows that the goal is specific; there is a goal for the content learning intention and the SEL learning intention.

- **Measurable:** The goal uses both quantitative and qualitative measurements with consideration of the content learning intention and the SEL learning intention. The example in figure 7.1 shows that the goal uses a quantitative measurement to show growth in the content learning intention and a qualitative measurement to show growth in the SEL learning intention.

- **Attainable:** The goal is practical and fits within the context of one year's growth in one year's time. The example demonstrates that the goal is attainable because it is established to show growth within the allotted duration of this unit.

- **Results oriented:** The goal is based on the qualities and characteristics we want from ideal graduates.

- **Time bound:** The goal is within the context of one unit of study and considering one year's growth in one year's time. In addition, not only is it time bound regarding the end goal for the unit, but it also has clear protocols to implement using formative student data *during* the unit.

In addition to ensuring that the SPBL process focuses on evidence of student learning and quality student work, goal setting promotes sustainability in that the ultimate goal for the unit is to ensure evidence of student growth. Earlier in the book, I explored the evolution of a relationship with PBL (see figure 3.2, page 44). That graphic depicts the difference between focusing on fidelity to the model and focusing on the integrity of student learning. The goal-setting step of the SPBL process is imperative in growing teachers' efficacy and ensuring that teachers focus on both the fidelity of PBL implementation and the integrity of the learning taking place.

Figure 7.1 shows an example template for developing your SPBL unit learning goal. Consider the following as you develop your goal.

1. The focus is on evidence of learning for both the content and SEL learning intentions.

2. The SMART goal format allows the goal to be specific, measurable, attainable, results oriented, and time bound.

3. The assessment calendar is used to determine what formative assessments you will analyze throughout the process (warm-up questions, weekly quizzes, and project milestones).

4. The goals show an equal amount of respect for both qualitative data (to assess SEL skills) and quantitative data (to assess content knowledge).

5. Protocols are predetermined to ensure there is a commitment to what milestones, formative assessments, or other student learning artifacts will be discussed to determine if students are growing in their knowledge, understanding, and application (surface, deep, transfer) of the academic and SEL learning intentions. (If you are working with a team of teachers, determine what specific protocols you will use. If you are working individually, simply solidify the learning artifacts you will check throughout the process.)

	Explanation	Plan
SPBL SMART Goal Template		
1. Content learning intention: I can apply the knowledge I gain from historical research on the causes of the U.S. Civil War to create connections and solutions.		
2. SEL learning intention (social awareness): I can present the perspective of another race on an issue of discrimination.		
Strategic and Specific	The goal is direct and detailed.	**Content goal:** All students will show quantitative evidence of growth between the pre- and postassessments. All students will score an 80 percent or higher on the quantitative postassessment. Common formative assessments to analyze this goal using a protocol are: • Weekly quiz on abolitionists (see the What? So What? Now What? Protocol, appendix B, page 142) • Milestone 3, the compare-and-contrast chart (see the Examining Student Work Protocol, appendix B, page 143)
Measurable	The goal uses both quantitative and qualitative measurements with consideration of the content learning intention and the SEL learning intention.	
Attainable	The goal is practical and fits within the context of one year's growth in one year's time.	
Results Oriented	The goal is based on the qualities and characteristics we want from ideal graduates.	**SEL goal:** All students will grow in their understanding of the concept of social awareness. They will be able to take on the perspective of those with opposing viewpoints and exhibit empathy for those who have been impacted by modern-day slavery or unethical labor practices. Growth in this goal will be measured qualitatively through the culminating public product rubric, class discussions, and written reflections.
Time Bound	The goal is within the context of one unit of study. The goal is made with the consideration of at least one year's growth in one year's time.	A common formative assessment to analyze this goal using a protocol is a random sampling of a few journal entries to check students' understanding of empathy or perspective (see the Tuning Protocol, appendix B, page 144).

Figure 7.1: SPBL SMART goal template example.

*Visit **go.SolutionTree.com/21stcenturyskills** for a free blank reproducible version of this figure.*

This SMART goal template models the *how* in establishing a learning goal to measure student learning growth during the SPBL unit. The first few times you implement step 3 in the SPBL process, you might use this SMART goal template. After you have gone through the process a few times, create a revised template that works for you and your team The outcome of step 3 in the SPBL process is the evidence of student learning through a clear goal. Having a goal, as depicted in figure 7.1 (page 103) allows teachers to answer the three SPBL questions (CASEL, n.d.b).

1. How do you ensure at least one year's growth in one year's time?

2. How do you ensure an equal intensity of surface-, deep-, and transfer-level learning for each unit of study?

3. How do you define and provide intentional feedback to students on their growth in both content knowledge and SEL skills?

Answering these three questions is a nonnegotiable when it comes to SPBL. The SMART goal format provides a template to organize thoughts around answering those three questions. Some might view the SMART goal format as too cumbersome or restrictive. Perhaps you can start with the SMART goal template for a few units and then create a customized goal-setting template that works best for you and your students.

As long as teachers craft their template with the end goal of answering the three SPBL questions, they have the autonomy to choose how to approach crafting the goals. Two important aspects of setting effective SMART goals are to collaborate with colleagues and consider how you apply quantitative versus qualitative metrics.

As you and your colleagues work through step 3 of the SPBL process, there are a few strategies to consider to enhance the goal-setting process, including intentional collaboration with colleagues, quantitative and qualitative data collection, achievement measures versus growth measures, and using protocols to enhance conversations around learning goals.

Collaboration With Colleagues

Perhaps you are in a situation in which you do not have the structure or opportunity to collaborate with colleagues who teach the same grade level or subject matter. If this is the case, work individually to create a goal that you and your students can monitor. However, if you do have the opportunity to collaborate with colleagues, this is ideal.

Crafting a clear and measurable goal with a team and accomplishing or meeting that goal are what builds collective teacher efficacy. Crafting a goal that measures growth in both content knowledge and an SEL skill has the potential to be even more rewarding.

Quantitative and Qualitative Data Collection

Recall from chapter 6 (page 87) that SPBL promotes the use of both quantitative and qualitative assessments to measure growth and provide practical feedback to students. In the SPBL model, you will use more quantitative measurements to assess growth in the content learning intention, specifically for surface and deep levels of knowledge, and more qualitative measurements to assess growth in the SEL learning intention.

Note that there is a content goal and an SEL goal. Developing the SMART goal ensures that there is both quantitative and qualitative evidence of growth. It also provides a clear vision for growth in the designated SEL skill. It is important to note that step 3 of the SPBL process is simply creating the goal. In step 4 (chapter 8, page 109), you will learn about implementing the goal through teacher action research.

Achievement Measures Versus Growth Measures

When teachers measure *achievement*, they are typically measuring how well students do against a specific standard or compared to other students. When they measure *growth*, they are measuring students compared to themselves. Both measuring achievement and measuring growth are important to implement, but also important to distinguish when crafting your SPBL goal.

The content goal in figure 7.1 (page 103) shows an example of an achievement goal: "All students will show quantitative evidence of growth between the pre- and postassessments. All students will score an 80 percent or higher on the quantitative postassessment." This is the quantitative measurement. This is a traditional goal that a teacher team might craft. It is measuring the overall achievement average for all students. Chapter 6 (page 87) shows a quantitative assessment (see figure 6.3, page 93), which depicts a traditional assessment gauging students' surface and deep knowledge The assessment is also a common assessment, so it serves as a measurement for all of the eighth grade social studies teachers in the building. The design and scoring of this test make it easy for teachers to provide students with a preassessment and a postassessment and track growth and achievement for both individual students and an entire class or course.

The challenge of crafting a goal around an SEL skill is that it is difficult to quantify. However, clearly defining the SEL skill, developing a clear learning intention and success criteria, and having a vision of what an exemplar looks, sounds, and feels like make creating a rubric for an SEL skill easier, as depicted in the culminating public product rubric in figure 6.1 (page 90). Once you establish a common rubric, measuring both growth and achievement becomes easier.

The example SEL goal in figure 7.1 (page 103) is "All students will grow in their understanding of the concept of social awareness. They will be able to take on the perspective of those with opposing viewpoints and exhibit empathy for those who have been impacted by modern-day slavery or unethical labor practices." Teachers can *qualitatively* measure growth in this goal through the culminating public product rubric, class discussions, and written reflections. It makes sense when assessing SEL to prioritize assessment based on individual growth, as there are no data to glean from comparing students to each other for acquisition of SEL skills. In SEL, students are only seeking to grow as individuals.

Another strategy to consider as you contemplate achievement measures versus growth measures is the idea of reassessment or retakes. If a student does not do well on a quantitative summative assessment, and if your team agrees in the inherent SPBL philosophy of ensuring student growth (at least one year's growth in one year's time), then you should give students the opportunity to reassess their learning. Granted, you should establish specific parameters prior to students earning the retake, such as, the student must complete all the unit milestones and quizzes. And perhaps the student must take the initiative to meet with you at some point prior to the reassessment. These are just example parameters, but they should encourage students to take some initiative to relearn material. This process encourages student growth in learning.

Protocols to Enhance Conversations Around Learning Goals

Part of growing collective teacher efficacy involves having strategic and intentional conversations about evidence of learning during teacher collaboration time. Sometimes, teachers are hesitant to use protocols because they feel too restrictive or formal, but using protocols allows educators to have more honest and more efficient conversations. You might challenge your colleagues to try using protocols in a few meetings, and then decide if your conversations are more honest and more efficient and go deeper in discussing student learning.

Hammond (2020) addresses the value of protocols well when she writes the following.

> I encourage teachers to find talk structures and tools that—
>
> - Honor the funds of knowledge each student brings to the conversation.
> - Give marginalized students greater access to the flow of the discussion.
> - Give students more agency in directing the conversation.
> - Give students a more robust cognitive workout by leveraging their everyday modes of communication.
>
> That's why I suggest a good starting point for facilitating deeper, more equitable discussions is to use structured protocols. (p. 46)

Figure 7.1 (page 103) clearly identifies common formative assessments for teachers to discuss through protocols (featured in chapter 8, page 109). Protocols allow for more honest and efficient conversations around learning.

Figure 7.2 shows the checklist for step 3 of the SPBL process. You can use this checklist for reflection as you create clear nonnegotiables for setting a goal for both content and SEL skills.

Checklist for Establishing a Clear Goal for Student Learning

☐ The focus is on evidence of learning for both the content and SEL learning intentions.

☐ The SMART goal format allows the goal to be specific, measurable, attainable, results oriented, and time bound.

☐ The assessment calendar is used to determine what formative assessments you will analyze throughout the process (warm-up questions, weekly quizzes, and project milestones).

☐ The goal shows an equal amount of respect for both qualitative data (to assess SEL skills) and quantitative data (to assess content knowledge).

☐ Protocols are predetermined to ensure there is a commitment to what milestones, formative assessments, or other student learning artifacts will be discussed to determine if students are growing in their knowledge, understanding, and application (surface, deep, transfer) of the academic and SEL learning intentions. (If you are working with a team of teachers, determine what specific protocols you will use. If you are working individually, simply solidify the learning artifacts you will check throughout the process.)

Figure 7.2: Checklist for establishing a clear goal for student learning.

*Visit **go.SolutionTree.com/21stcenturyskills** for a free reproducible version of this figure.*

Tips for Establishing a Clear Goal for Student Learning

Following are some helpful tips for creating clear goals focused on student learning.

- Genuinely consider each of the five elements of the SMART goals format (strategic and specific, measurable, attainable, results oriented, and time bound).

- SPBL is about placing equal value on the content learning intention and the SEL learning intention, which is why you should have a goal for each.

- Use protocols to analyze both quantitative and qualitative data. Using protocols ensures that everyone on the teacher team has an opportunity to contribute to the discussion.

- Make sure the team determines the common formative assessments to ground the conversation in growth along the way. Depending on practicality, some or all of the common formative assessments will be the focus for protocol discussions.

- If working individually, make sure that you have clear milestones and formative assessments sprinkled throughout the unit to ensure ongoing evidence and growth in learning.

Summary

Creating a clear goal focused on evidence of student learning is beneficial because it ensures teachers focus on the integrity of actual student learning rather than their fidelity to the PBL methodology. Another benefit of creating a clear goal for each unit is that it promotes deep and meaningful teacher collaboration. A clear goal focused on student growth in both academic content knowledge and an SEL skill can lead to strong collective teacher efficacy. To help promote this dialogue around the evidence of student learning, teachers should use protocols. Protocols are beneficial because they make conversations more honest and efficient, and they ensure teacher accountability for following through on implementation of the goal.

Questions for Reflection

Individually or in collaborative teams, answer the following questions to reflect on your learning in this chapter.

1. Will you or your team use the SMART goal format or a different format to create your content and SEL goals? Why?

2. How might you use quantitative data to measure student growth in the content learning intention and qualitative data to measure student growth in the SEL learning intention?

3. How do you feel about the three SPBL questions as they relate to your goal? Do you have an equal intensity and implementation of surface-, deep-, and transfer-level learning? How are you working toward the idea of one year's growth in one year's time?

Challenge

Make sure you are absolutely clear on what formative assessments you will be discussing throughout the process. Brainstorm a way to quantitatively measure student growth in an SEL skill.

CHAPTER 8

STEP 4: CONDUCTING TEACHER ACTION RESEARCH

Now that your team has a clear learning goal, it's time to create your plan for teacher action research, a key component that sets SPBL apart from PBL. Educational authors Richard D. Parsons and Kimberlee S. Brown (2002) define *teacher action research* as:

> A form of investigation designed for use by teachers to attempt to solve problems and improve professional practices in their classrooms. It involves systematic observations and data collection, which can then be used by the practitioner-researcher in reflection, decision making, and the development of more effective classroom strategies. (p. 4)

Earlier in the book, I noted that Hattie's research identifies collective teacher efficacy as having a significant impact on student learning. Collective teacher efficacy can be defined as "the shared belief by a group of teachers in a particular educational environment that they have the skills to positively impact student outcomes" (Visible Learning Meta^X, n.d.).

In other words, when a team of teachers sets a goal for student learning and believes they can achieve that goal, Hattie's research indicates that it has an effect size of 1.36 (Visible Learning Meta^X, n.d.). This is more than three year's growth in one years' time. As of August 2021, out of all of the 322 influences that Hattie researched, it finishes second only behind teacher estimates on student achievement.

Conducting teacher action research within the SPBL process is what teacher collective efficacy is all about. In traditional PBL, reflection during and at the end of the unit might be, "How well did we implement the seven PBL design elements?" In SPBL, teachers collectively work together to answer the three SPBL questions (see page 45) as they plan and implement SPBL units, forcing the focus on the student learning.

Teachers become action researchers during the SPBL process by using protocols around both quantitative and qualitative data and the three levels of learning (surface, deep, and transfer) as well as the targeted SEL competency to determine how they know students have learned. This involves ongoing observation and dialogue around the clear evidence of learning established in step 3 with the learning goal. Step 4, teacher action research, is implementing and tracking the progress toward the goal established in step 3. And, as noted earlier, this work is best done in collaborative teacher teams. In "Teachers as Researchers," Robert Marzano and colleagues (2020) state:

> There is no doubt that instructional change and improvement happens at the individual class and school level. However, school systems cannot achieve sustained improvement in teacher practice and student learning outcomes at any scale if it is solely dependent on the professional prowess of individual classroom teachers. Teacher collaboration has been gaining momentum because 10 teachers' participation in quality collaborative learning leads to enhanced human capital (knowledge, skills, attitudes), which helps spread change and improvement throughout the system. (p. 8)

Within the context of the SPBL process, teachers should ground every goal, every protocol, and every conversation in the three SPBL questions (CASEL, n.d.b). So, no matter what goal, meeting agenda, or protocol you choose in your action research, understand that the purpose of all the SPBL action research process is grounded in discussing and answering those three questions.

This chapter explains the *action* in action research. It reviews specific high-impact strategies and how they connect with SPBL and examines a variety of protocols that teacher teams can use to discuss student data and conduct teacher-to-teacher observations. Finally, it discusses ideas for increasing awareness to promote equity within the context of the action research. In this chapter, I continue to use the eighth-grade SPBL anchor unit, and when I talk about the action research team or teacher team, I am referencing all eighth grade social studies teachers; they are the action research team.

The *Action* in Action Research

Once your team chooses and implements an action research protocol, team members use the research to adjust and adapt instruction. These protocols must always result in an *action*. It is imperative that teachers make instructional adjustments based on the action research during the SPBL process. The SPBL process encourages educators to ask more poignant reflective questions to help them make critical decisions about adapting their instruction. As the research indicates individual gaps in student learning, the following questions can help frame instructional adjustments.

- Based on the data, are individual students struggling with surface-, deep-, or transfer-level learning?

- What high-impact strategies might you use to enhance learning (see figure 1.4, page 14)?

- Are students struggling because they do not have clarity about the learning intentions and success criteria? If so, how might students and teachers co-construct the success criteria together?

- Is a lack of interest or engagement leading to learning gaps? If so, how might you adjust the PBL equalizer to increase engagement (see figure 2.11, page 36)? How might incorporating specific high-impact strategies within the context of the seven PBL elements enhance student learning?

- How are students increasing in their knowledge and awareness of the SEL learning intention?

If you are in the middle of your SPBL unit, and students are not learning at the level you think they should be, and the milestones or formative assessments simply are not displaying the growth you had hoped, you can use figure 8.1 as a cheat sheet to remind you of high-impact strategies and how they connect with the elements of PBL. Use trial and error if you need to achieve the evidence of learning or the goal you created in step 3.

Influence	Effect Size	Primary PBL Essential Element Connection	What It Looks Like in the SPBL Classroom
Teacher clarity	0.84	Key knowledge and success skills	Students are clear on where they are in their learning (surface, deep, and transfer).
Self-judgment and reflection	0.75	Critique and revision	Students use specific self-feedback and peer feedback protocols throughout the unit.
Reciprocal teaching	0.74	Reflection	Students read texts they predict, question, clarify, and summarize.
Summarization	0.74	Reflection	Students consistently and individually journal about their learning.
Problem-solving teaching	0.67	Authenticity or challenging problem or question	Students reference the driving question and consult outside experts to provide unique perspectives in helping them generate their own answer to the driving question.
Creativity programs	0.58	Student voice and choice	Students have choice in a specific role or a product they produce and create.

Source: Adapted from Visible Learning Meta^X, n.d.

Figure 8.1: Connections between Hattie's high-impact strategies and elements of PBL.

These high-impact strategies serve as not only a tool to use when you need to adjust instruction during your SPBL unit, but it also shows the direct correlation between high-impact strategies and the seven PBL design elements. Being intentional about using high-impact strategies within the context of the seven PBL design elements is one of the characteristics that sets SPBL apart from PBL.

Figure 8.2 shows the checklist for step 4 of the PBL process, conducting teacher action research. This list provides clear nonnegotiables for conducting teacher action research.

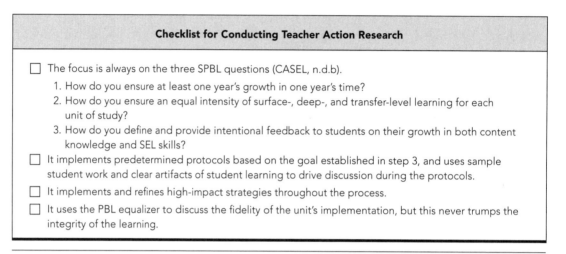

Checklist for Conducting Teacher Action Research

☐ The focus is always on the three SPBL questions (CASEL, n.d.b).
   1. How do you ensure at least one year's growth in one year's time?
   2. How do you ensure an equal intensity of surface-, deep-, and transfer-level learning for each unit of study?
   3. How do you define and provide intentional feedback to students on their growth in both content knowledge and SEL skills?
☐ It implements predetermined protocols based on the goal established in step 3, and uses sample student work and clear artifacts of student learning to drive discussion during the protocols.
☐ It implements and refines high-impact strategies throughout the process.
☐ It uses the PBL equalizer to discuss the fidelity of the unit's implementation, but this never trumps the integrity of the learning.

Figure 8.2: Checklist for conducting teacher action research.

*Visit **go.SolutionTree.com/21stcenturyskills** for a free reproducible version of this figure.*

Being able to effectively talk about clear evidence of student learning is a significant aspect of the teacher action research process. Again, using protocols during teacher action research is an important aspect of SPBL.

Protocols to Analyze Evidence of Learning

In the discussion of SMART goals in chapter 7 (page 101), you learned that there are agreed-on protocols established for each SMART goal and each unit. Your team should decide which protocols to use to discuss and analyze student work within the goal. For example, the What? So What? Now What? Protocol is effective for examining quantitative data, such as a spreadsheet with a class list of pre- and post-test scores from a summative assessment of surface and deep learning. The Examining Student Work Protocol works well for analyzing a more qualitative student learning artifact. The Tuning Protocol works well for examining randomly sampled student products. You will find examples of these protocols in this chapter, along with reproducible versions and more, in appendix B (page 141).

The teacher action research team for the anchor unit used the What? So What? Now What? Protocol to examine quantitative data collected from the abolitionist multiple-choice quiz. The team discussed the SEL goal similarly to the way they discussed the content goal.

Review the SEL goal from chapter 7 (figure 7.1, page 103): "All students will grow in their understanding of the concept of social awareness. They will be able to take on the perspective of those with opposing viewpoints and exhibit empathy for those who have been impacted by modern-day slavery or unethical labor practices." You can measure this goal qualitatively through the culminating public product rubric, class discussions, and written reflections.

Figure 8.3 is an example of what the What? So What? Now What? Protocol would look like when implemented during a team meeting. You should use this protocol with students at some point when they might be reflecting on their own work or examining something else.

	What the Presenter Does	What the Audience Does	Time Allotted
What?	Explains the quantitative or qualitative data Explains the content learning intention and success criteria Explains what level of learning it represents (surface, deep, or transfer) and why	Listens and takes notes using sentence stems like the following: • I liked . . . • I wonder . . . • I suggest . . . • Questions this raises for me in my own work include . . .	Four minutes
So What?	Sits down, listens, and takes notes on audience feedback	Verbally shares notes generated in the What?, using the same sentence stems: • I liked . . . • I wonder . . . • I suggest . . . • Questions this raises for me in my own work include . . .	Four minutes
Now What?	Explains how the feedback resonated and what next steps might be	Listens	Three minutes
Total time:			Eleven minutes

Source: Adapted from Gene Thompson-Grove, 2017.

Figure 8.3: What? So What? Now What? Protocol.

You can use the Examining Student Work Protocol in figure 8.4 (page 114) to review qualitative data collected from milestone 3 in the anchor unit (the compare-and-contrast chart).

Setup: 1. Review the protocol. 2. Establish the facilitator and timekeeper.	Two minutes
Presenter Actions: The presenter takes the following actions. 1. Presents the project context and driving question 2. Describes the teaching and learning context and standards or learning targets 3. Describes how the essential PBL elements were incorporated into the project 4. Describes the best teaching practices and protocols used throughout the project 5. Shares materials related to learning and student work 6. Poses one or two focus questions about the teaching and learning that took place	Ten minutes
Clarifying Questions by Participants: Participants ask nonevaluative questions about the project using the language from the culminating public product rubric.	Three minutes
Individual Silent Writing: Participants review notes about the presentation and record thoughts on how to address the focus questions. • What did the students do well? • What evidence exists in the work samples to support this?	Three minutes
Participant Discussion While the Presenter Takes Notes (Round-Robin Style): For each round, use the following sentence stems: Round 1: "I noticed . . ." or "I observed . . ." Round 2: "I wonder . . ." Round 3: "In the future, consider . . ."	Nine minutes
Debriefing: The presenter discusses the feedback and identifies areas of success and challenge within the unit.	Three minutes
Total time:	Thirty minutes

Source: Adapted from Baron, 2017.

Figure 8.4: Examining Student Work Protocol.

You can use the Tuning Protocol in figure 8.5 to examine randomly sampled journal entries to gauge student understanding of empathy or perspective. Just as you would do for the content learning intention, as a teacher team, establish and discuss an exemplar for an SEL learning intention's common formative assessment or learning artifact. This exemplar is based on the success criteria (established during step 1 in chapter 5, page 69).

Presentation	Presenter presents qualitative or quantitative evidence of learning.	Five minutes
Clarification	Audience asks a clarifying question (for example, "Can you please repeat the learning intention?").	One minute
I Liked Statements	Presenter listens (even turns their back to the audience to focus on listening to the feedback and not reading body language or facial expressions) and takes notes. Audience discusses specific aspects of the artifact and presentation they like.	Three minutes
I Wonder Statements	Presenter listens (remains turned around if comfortable) and continues to take notes. Audience discusses possible areas of development.	Three minutes
Possible Next Steps	Presenter listens (remains turned around if comfortable) and continues to take notes. Audiences discusses specific suggested next steps.	Three minutes
Reflection	Presenter turns around and discusses what feedback they found helpful.	Three minutes
Open Discussion	Presenter and audience members have an open discussion sharing additional ideas and resources.	Two minutes
Total time:		Twenty minutes

Source: Adapted from School Reform Initiative, 2017c.

Figure 8.5: Tuning Protocol.

The three protocols outlined in figures 8.3, 8.4, and 8.5 (pages 113–115) are the protocols the teacher team agreed on and established in the SMART goal from step 3. However, once you and your team members feel comfortable and have a high level of trust, consider using protocols to observe one another in each other's classrooms, such as the Lesson Study Protocol or the Focused Observation Protocol (see appendix B, page 141).

Again, it is important to note that these protocols are used as examples. I selected them to build on the example established with the SMART goals in chapter 7 (page 101). However, which protocols you use and *how* you put them to use should vary based on your collaborative needs, the nature of the SPBL projects you're undertaking, and your students' specific needs. If your team decides that using the specific protocols provided in this book (see appendix B, page 141) is too restrictive, not only should you adjust aspects of these protocols such as the time spent in each step, but use these as guides to create your own. Creating your own protocols allows your team to have complete ownership of the process.

Figure 8.6 (page 116) offers strategies for creating your own action research protocol.

Strategies for Creating an Action Research Protocol
• All team members have an equal opportunity to share ideas.
• Team discussions are focused on the three SPBL questions.
• Members discuss both quantitative and qualitative data.
• All team members have the opportunity to speak their truth within the context of the protocol.
• The team determines clear actions and next steps as a result of the protocol.
• The team establishes specific time frames in an effort to keep the conversation focused and efficient.

Figure 8.6: Strategies for creating an action research protocol.

*Visit **go.SolutionTree.com/21stcenturyskills** for a free reproducible version of this figure.*

Teacher action research should include protocols to promote equity within conversations. Equity is an important theme as you conduct teacher action research not just within team discussions, but also in how team members view and interpret student data.

Equity in Teacher Action Research

Like most people, I have my own implicit biases and perspectives, and I personally strive to continue to challenge my own assumptions and grow in my self-awareness and social awareness. I recognize that at times when talking about equity, specifically racial equity, although my intent might be good, my actions and impact do not align with my intent. My intent will always be to meet the needs of all students, and to work to promote an equitable learning environment. I do believe, however, that if our goal, as educators, is to meet the needs of *all* students, then we need to lean into conversations about equity, which sometimes can make us feel uncomfortable.

I have worked with schools in which teacher teams used a chart similar to the one in figure 8.7. If used incorrectly, and without clear norms and guidelines, this chart could potentially promote stereotyping and decrease teacher self-awareness, which would be the exact opposite of its purpose. I also have worked in some schools in which teacher teams noticed that there were significant discrepancies and inequities in certain areas not previously identified.

	Asian or Pacific Islander	Black	Hispanic	White	Multiracial	Indigenous	Native American
Total number of students							
Total number of students with 504 plans							
Percentage of students with 504 plans							

Total number of students with individual language plans (ILPs)							
Percentage of students with ILPs							
Total number of students with individual education plans (IEPs)							
Percentage of students with IEPs							
Total number of students with D and F grades							
Percentage of students with Ds or Fs							
Total number of students with Advanced Placement or International Baccalaureate course selections for the following year							
Percentage of Advanced Placement or International Baccalaureate course selections for the following year							

Source: Adapted from © 2021 by Justin Quick. Used with permission.

Figure 8.7: Subgroup data breakdown chart.

As educators, we have an obligation to teach *all* students. When we sign our contract at a public school, we commit to working as hard as we can to ensure students of all backgrounds, circumstances, and identities reach their full potential. At times, this might force us to recognize some of our own biases and gaps in understanding, and work collectively with our colleagues to have ongoing dialogue about meeting the needs of all students.

In *Courageous Conversations About Race*, Singleton and Linton (2022) state that there are four agreements of courageous conversations:

1. Stay engaged: "Participants are not allowed to 'check out' of the conversation. They must remain morally, emotionally, intellectually, and socially involved in the dialogue" (p. 59).

2. Experience discomfort: "Participants need to be willing to engage in dialogue authenti-cally. Participants need to be personally responsible for pushing themselves, which might make them uncomfortable but lead to real growth" (p. 63).

3. Speak your truth: "Be absolutely honest about the thoughts, feelings, and opinions that you have. You should not just say what you think people want to hear" (p. 60).

4. Expect and accept non-closure: "The solution is revealed in the process of dialogue itself. Issues of racial equity are complex. 'If people expect and accept non-closure in racial dis-course, then the more they talk, the more they learn; and the more they learn, the more appropriate and promising will be their actions and interventions'" (p. 65).

You and your team members can apply these four agreements when meeting throughout the SPBL process to discuss your action research. These norms or agreements are especially important because teacher action research in SPBL can prove to be an opportunity to lean into equity for students, equity in participation and conversations should also be modeled among teachers.

Consider One Student's Perspective

One idea for increasing self-awareness of equity among students is to have your teacher action research team members take on a student's perspective. In her article, "Four Tools to Interrupt Implicit Bias," Hammond (2015b) states:

> Perspective-taking involves stepping into the shoes of a stereotyped person. What does it feel like to have your intelligence automatically questioned, or to be trailed by detectives each time you walk into a store? Perspective-taking can be very useful in assessing the emotional impact on individuals who are constantly being stereotyped in negative ways. It is also a way to checking one's self if you begin to judge a person of color for reacting a particular way in a stressful situation.

Ask team members to think about one student they have in class. Consider that student's strengths, areas of improvement, and what life is like at home. Consider where this student might need support within the context of the SPBL unit. Consider what scaffolds might need to be put in place. Once each individual teacher on the team has completed this exercise indi-vidually, have everyone share their thoughts on what they came up with.

Analyze Student Demographic Data

In an ongoing effort to increase awareness of meeting the needs of all students, I encourage teacher teams to incorporate student subgroup data into their conversations. But in doing so, be aware that true, long-lasting change boils down to being genuinely self-motivated to interrupt implicit bias. Looking at student demographic data might only result in generating initial awareness of implicit bias that might exist. However, doing it within the context of SPBL teacher action research, that research might not only increase awareness of implicit bias, but pro-mote a clear action to implementing instruction that promotes culturally responsive teaching (Lucas Education Research, 2021).

With all this in mind, and knowing that the intent of looking at student demographic data might be helpful to create initial awareness of implicit bias, and determining some ways to approach addressing these gaps, consider the following.

- Grade distribution broken down by ethnicity
- Grade distribution for students who are English learners
- Grade distribution for students who have 504 plans
- Grade distribution for students who have individualized learning plans (ILPs) or individualized education programs (IEPs)
- Instead of just grade distribution data, evidence of surface-, deep-, and transfer-level learning for all these subgroups

Having these subgroup data can help further answer and address the three SPBL questions. When discussing evidence of learning for these subgroups, it is imperative that teachers approach the data by first reflecting on their own teaching practices and focusing on what is within their control as a teacher to enhance the learning of all students.

Another tool or approach for promoting equity and courageous conversations about race from Singleton and Linton (2022) is the courageous conversations compass. The authors describe the compass as follows:

> On this compass, we have identified four primary ways that people process racial information, events, or issues: moral, intellectual, emotional, and social. These are the four points or cardinal directions of our compass. Those positioned in the moral quadrant develop a deep-seated belief related to the racial information or event. This belief has to do with the "rightness" or "wrongness" of any given issue. One's justifications for a moral viewpoint are often located in the "gut," and articulating them verbally may not be possible. On an intellectual level, the primary response to a racial issue or information is characterized by a personal disconnect from the subject or a steadfast search for additional information or data. The intellectual response is often verbal and based on one's thinking. In the emotional arena, educators respond to information through feelings in the sense that a racial issue strikes them at a physical level causing an internal sensation such as anger, sadness, joy, or embarrassment. Finally, a view positioned in the social zone of the compass reveals one's connection and response to racial information through doing, as defined by specific behaviors and actions. In a sense, moral responses reside in the soul, intellectual in the mind, emotional in the heart, and social in our hands and feet. (pp. 135–136)

The compass aligns moral responses with personal beliefs, intellectual responses with thinking, emotional responses with feelings, and social responses with doing.

Overall, the SPBL framework provides opportunities for equity, emphasizes student voice and choice, and empowers students by addressing authentic, real-world problems. SPBL also gives teachers an opportunity to have conversations about the evidence of learning for all students. These conversations might be difficult, but using Singleton and Linton's (2022) four courageous conversation agreements and being mindful of Hammond's (2015b) ideas about self-motivation in addressing implicit bias, can help your teams have valuable conversations that lean into equity when conducting teacher action research.

Tips for Conducting Teacher Action Research

Following are some helpful tips for conducting teacher action research.

- If your team gets confused at any point about conducting teacher action research, simply do two things: (1) refer back to your goal from step 3, and (2) reference the three SPBL questions (see page 45).

- Your team should challenge themselves to grow and lean into dialogue about student learning that at times might be uncomfortable. In those cases, reference Singleton and Linton's (2022) four courageous conversation agreements.

Summary

Step 4 of the SPBL implementation process is focused on teacher action research. This step is about implementing the established goal and focusing on the three key SPBL questions. This step ensures that teacher teams use protocols that result in more honest and efficient conversations with a focus on student work and evidence of learning. Teams can use pre-created protocols or create a protocol themselves to create equity around this research.

Questions for Reflection

Individually or in collaborative teams, answer the following questions to reflect on your learning in this chapter.

1. Why should teachers consider implementing protocols during collaboration time?

2. What are the benefits of incorporating teacher action research?

3. Out of the three SPBL questions, which one is most challenging for your team to discuss? Why?

4. Action research is a vital aspect of the SPBL process. What will your team do to ensure team members have enough trust to participate in an effective action research process (for example, observe one another using a critique protocol)?

Challenge

Consider using one of the protocols, such as the Lesson Study Protocol (see appendix B, page 141), to observe another teacher implementing SPBL practices in the classroom and gauge the evidence of learning. Are students meeting the learning intention? Can students state the success criteria at each of the three levels of learning?

CHAPTER 9

STEP 5: REFLECTING, REFINING, AND CELEBRATING

Once you and your team complete step 4, teacher action research, and the students have met the learning goals, demonstrating surface, deep, and transfer levels of learning, and once they have answered the driving question and presented their culminating public product, it's time to reflect, refine, and celebrate the authentic and meaningful learning experience. Reflecting, refining, and celebrating is for both students and teachers. Often, these are three things we, as educators, do not take time to do, and often, they can be the most important.

Reflection

As stated previously, reflection is one of the PBL design elements. Reflection should not only occur throughout the unit but also on completion of the unit. Famous educational constructivist author John Dewey (1933) wrote:

> Of course intellectual learning includes the amassing and retention of information. But information is an undigested burden unless it is understood. It is knowledge only as its material is comprehended. And understanding, comprehension, means that the various parts of the information acquired are grasped in their relations to one another—a result that is attained only when acquisition is accompanied by constant reflection upon the meaning of what is studied. (pp. 78–79)

To paraphrase, one does not learn from experience; one learns from *reflecting* on experience.

Teachers have three aspects of experience to reflect on at the end of the SPBL process.

1. **The integrity of student learning:** Reflecting on students' level of learning is far more important than reflecting on fidelity to the SPBL process. Ensure the learning is the

priority by consistently discussing the three SPBL questions. For example, revisit the SPBL goal you developed in step 3. Were the goals met? Why or why not? What do some of the student-completed milestones look like? And how do they represent the three levels of learning?

2. **Negotiable and nonnegotiable aspects of the SPBL process:** Review the negotiable and nonnegotiable aspects of the SPBL process in table 3.1 (page 45). How well did you or your team do? Ask, "What tight principles were you or your team successful in implementing? How might we enhance these principles for next time?"

3. **The SPBL process itself:** Consider the five steps of the SPBL process. As you gain experience with this process, perhaps you or your team begin to use the nonnegotiable and negotiable SPBL principles to create a modified or entirely different method or cycle. This is OK. Ultimately, each school and community has different needs and different goals. As you gain experience with this process, it is inevitable that you will find ways to improve on it for your specific use cases. Hopefully, this means that everyone involved has significant ownership and input to enhance learning experiences for students.

Remember, the five steps of the SPBL process are intended to provide guidance and structure to answer the three SPBL questions (see page 45). Use your answers to these questions to determine specific refinements to your approach, as discussed in the next section.

Refinement

After your team has reflected on the process, use the data from the full range of assessments and the culminating public product to help make decisions for your next SPBL unit.

Consider the following questions.

- What adjustments do you need to make to your learning intentions and success criteria?

- What adjustments do you need to make to your unit design? Do you include more or fewer PBL elements?

- How might you increase student ownership, voice, and choice in the process (for example, have students develop the driving question and success criteria)?

- How might you enhance the use of high-yield strategies?

- How might you enhance the use of protocols for both teacher team meetings and student team meetings?

- As you consider all the conversations around learning you had as a team during this process, how might you guide students to have similar conversations about their learning and the process of learning in class?

Figure 9.1 shows the checklists for each step of the SPBL process, including new checklists for step 5. Use these checklists to reflect on and refine your SPBL process.

Step 1: Plan the SPBL Unit	Checklist
Stage 1: Create a learning intention for both academic content and SEL.	Learning intentions: ☐ Are written in clear, student-friendly language (*I can . . . , I will . . .*) ☐ Are written at the transfer level (application) ☐ Make it so the context can be applied to another context ☐ Clearly connect content and social and emotional learning
Stage 2: Develop content and SEL success criteria for each level of learning (surface, deep, and transfer).	Success criteria: ☐ Provide the ingredients to meet the learning intention ☐ Focus on learning at each level (surface, deep, and transfer) rather than tasks or activities ☐ Can be articulated by students ☐ Align to exemplars and models that address quality ☐ Allow students some level of ownership in crafting them
Stage 3: Craft the driving question at the transfer level, adding authentic context for the unit.	The driving question: ☐ Restates the learning intention as a question ☐ Is written at the transfer level (*To what extent . . . , When . . . , Who . . . , Where . . .*) ☐ Provides the "Why does this matter?" (authenticity) ☐ Adds context
Stage 4: Create tasks that align with the success criteria.	Tasks: ☐ Ensure students show evidence of learning at each level of complexity (surface, deep, and transfer) ☐ Include reading, writing, and speaking at each level of complexity ☐ Embed Hattie's high-impact strategies
Stage 5: Create an entry event to launch the sustained-inquiry process.	The entry event: ☐ Ensures student-generated need-to-know questions go to the heart of both the academic and SEL learning intentions ☐ Is embedded with the driving question ☐ Ensures students are clear about what learning transfer looks and sounds like ☐ Makes it so students are able to answer the question, "Why are we learning this?"
Step 2: Develop SPBL Assessments	**Checklist**
SPBL Culminating Public Product Rubric (see figure 6.1, page 90)	☐ It has the same and consistent success criteria based on the learning intention from the SPBL unit planner. This helps ensure clarity, consistency, practicality. ☐ There is a strong effort to ensure students demonstrate and equal intensity of all three levels of learning. ☐ The focus is more on the evidence of learning than the product.
Summative Assessment for Surface and Deep Learning (see figure 6.3, page 93)	☐ There is both a pre- and postassessment to measure student growth in their surface and deep levels of learning. ☐ The assessment is based on the determined surface- and deep-level success criteria from the SPBL unit planner.

Figure 9.1: Checklists for the SPBL process.

continued ▶

Anticipated Need-to-Know Map (see figure 6.5, page 94)	☐ It includes key milestones that allow for evidence of student learning at all three levels (surface, deep, and transfer), planning backward from the culminating public product. ☐ When designing the unit, generate the ideal need-to-knows you want students to ask at each level (surface, deep, and transfer) before each milestone (or phase of the unit). If students' anticipated need-to-knows surpass your expectations, adjust instruction accordingly. If the need-to-knows do not meet your expectations, adjust instruction accordingly (for example, implement some direct instruction).
Formative Assessment Calendar (see figure 6.7, page 97)	☐ It is like a traditional unit calendar planned backward from the culminating public product. ☐ It includes intentional surface, deep, and transfer assessments that are both quantitative (lead up to the summative assessment for surface and deep learning) and qualitative (lead up to the culminating public product rubric for transfer learning, often in the form of key milestones building up to the product).
Step 3: Establish a Clear Goal for Student Learning	**Checklist**
	☐ The goal is focused on evidence of learning for both the content and SEL learning intentions. ☐ The SMART goal format allows the goal to be specific, measurable, attainable, results oriented, and time bound. ☐ The assessment calendar is used to determine what formative assessments you will analyze throughout the process (warm-up questions, weekly quizzes, and project milestones). ☐ The goal shows an equal amount of respect for both qualitative data (to assess SEL skills) and quantitative data (to assess content knowledge). ☐ Protocols are predetermined to ensure there is a commitment to what milestones, formative assessments, or other student learning artifacts will be discussed to determine if students are growing in their knowledge, understanding, and application (surface, deep, transfer) of the academic and SEL learning intentions. (Note: If you are working with a team of teachers, determine what specific protocols you will use. If you are working individually, simply solidify the learning artifacts you will check throughout the process.)
Step 4: Conduct Teacher Action Research	**Checklist**
	☐ The focus is always on the three SPBL questions (CASEL, n.d.b). 　　1. How do you ensure at least one year's growth in one year's time? 　　2. How do you ensure an equal intensity of surface-, deep-, and transfer-level learning for each unit of study? 　　3. How do you define and provide intentional feedback to students on their growth in both content knowledge and SEL skills? ☐ It implements predetermined protocols based on the goal established in step 3, and uses sample student work and clear artifacts of student learning to drive discussion during the protocols. ☐ It implements and refines high-impact strategies throughout the process. ☐ It uses the PBL equalizer to discuss the fidelity of the unit's implementation, but this never trumps the integrity of the learning.

Step 5: Reflect, Refine, and Celebrate	Checklist
	Reflect
	☐ Ask yourself and your team the following questions.
	• Were the three SPBL questions answered? Why or why not?
	• Looking at the SPBL negotiable and nonnegotiable principles from table 3.1 (page 45), what were you and your team successful in implementing?
	Refine
	☐ Ask yourself and your team the following questions.
	• Did you use the data gleaned from the student assessments and your experiences to refine the process so students grow in their assessment capability and ownership of learning?
	• Did you use the data gleaned from student assessments and your experiences to refine the process so students have more ownership in planning the SPBL unit and action research goal-setting and implementation process? (For example, consider having students co-construct success criteria and the driving question. Consider planning an interdisciplinary SPBL unit.)
	• How might I incorporate more high-impact strategies within the context of the SPBL unit?
	Celebrate
	☐ With students:
	• At some point in the SPBL unit, gather feedback from students regarding how they like to celebrate (snacks, music, and so on).
	• After students complete the culminating public product, encourage students to celebrate the success of their learning.
	• Create opportunities for students to affirm one another.
	☐ With your team:
	• Find ways to give kind and specific affirmation to each member of the team.
	• Honor and recognize how the work was challenging but rewarding.

*Visit **go.SolutionTree.com/21stcenturyskills** for a free reproducible version of this figure.*

As part of reflecting on and refining the process, it's important to increase student voice and ownership throughout the experience. Previously, I discussed the value of students being able to self-assess. As educators, we want students to be able to identify their level of learning (surface, deep, or transfer). We want students spending the majority of their class time speaking the language of both content and SEL success criteria. Here are some effective ways to promote student ownership of learning.

1. **Have students co-construct the success criteria with you:** Identify the learning intention, and then show them exemplars. Have them write out what makes the exemplars successful. Once you have heard student voices and identified some of this language, have students categorize the language into surface, deep, and transfer. Provide students with the success criteria checklist (see figure 5.4, page 71) as a guide, and let them go to work! This allows students to have ownership of the success criteria and increases the amount of time they use success criteria language when they speak with each other.

2. **Have students co-construct the driving question:** Provide students with several resources addressing the learning intention but through different contexts. For example, using the sample unit discussed throughout this book (with the learning intention focused on historical research of the

U.S. Civil War and the context of modern-day slavery), you could provide students with three different articles: (1) an article about life as a slave on a U.S. plantation during the 1840s, (2) an article about child labor law violations that exist today, and (3) an excerpt from either William Lloyd Garrison's newspaper *The Liberator* or Harriet Beecher Stowe's (1853) novel *Uncle Tom's Cabin*.

Have students complete a Venn diagram comparing and contrasting the resource samples. Give students the checklist for crafting a driving question (see figure 5.7, page 75), and have them co-construct the driving question. Similar to having students co-construct the success criteria, having them co-construct the driving question allows them to have greater voice and choice, and ownership of the process. When the driving question is in students' own words, students are able to more easily recall and reflect on the question.

3. **Plan interdisciplinary SPBL units:** One of the goals of SPBL is to have an equal intensity of surface, deep, and transfer learning. Students can continually learn transfer if you involve them in interdisciplinary units of study. Figure 9.2 shows an example interdisciplinary unit plan (Storm Surge Project) created by three teachers at Essex North Shore Agricultural and Technical School located outside Boston, Massachusetts: (1) biology teacher Rose Young, (2) natural resources teacher Paul Crofts, and (3) electrical teacher Richard Whitaker. Note that they have three content learning intentions and integrate their success criteria and tasks. See appendix C (page 153) to find more example SPBL units across subject areas and grade levels.

SPBL Unit Plan: Storm Surge Project

Stage 1: Create a learning intention for both academic content and SEL (a major concept for the unit and a CASEL competency).

1. Content learning intention: I can apply knowledge of the interrelatedness of abiotic and biotic factors to analyze the direct and indirect effects of human activities and natural disasters on biodiversity, carrying capacity, and ecosystem health, providing solutions for reducing these impacts (HS-LS2-1, HS-LS2-2, HS-LS2-6, HS-LS2-7). (Young)

2. Content learning intentions (career technical education):

- I can analyze the impacts of storm surge on community resources and determine the roles different organizations play. (Crofts)
- I can analyze the impacts of storm surge on utilities and the departments responsible for resource management and maintenance. (Whitaker)

3. SEL learning intention (social awareness):

- I can present the impacts of just and unjust social norms as they pertain to environmental justice populations (for example, how people manage emergency situations at the individual and community levels).

Stage 2: Develop content and SEL success criteria for each level of learning (daily learning goals).		
Surface-Level Success Criteria for Content <ul><li>I can identify resources.</li><li>I can name cultural and environmental resources.</li><li>I can restate census data.</li><li>I can define and list abiotic and biotic factors.</li><li>I can list ways (good and bad) in which humans impact their environment.</li><li>I can define social justice populations.</li></ul>	**Deep-Level Success Criteria for Content** <ul><li>I can look at data sets together.</li><li>I can explain the distribution of resources in a resource area.</li><li>I can analyze more than one resource data set for meaning.</li><li>I can deconstruct reasons for current resource distribution.</li><li>I can draw conclusions by analyzing two data sets together.</li><li>I can determine averages in data sets and determine trends using graphical comparisons of data sets.</li><li>I can explain how limiting factors at any one time determine an ecosystem's carrying capacity.</li><li>I can argue with evidence the need for greater biodiversity in a changing environment.</li></ul>	**Transfer-Level Success Criteria for Content** <ul><li>I can predict the impact of climate change on humans and wildlife populations in different parts of the world.</li><li>I can present my research methods and conclusion to members of the communities and professionals.</li><li>I can evaluate and refine a solution for reducing the impacts of human activities on biodiversity and ecosystem health.</li><li>I can make analogies between ecosystems and social systems.</li></ul>
Surface-Level Success Criteria for SEL <ul><li>I can name environmental justice populations.</li><li>I can define different levels of economic status.</li><li>I can restate that abiotic and biotic resources play a role in environmental justice.</li><li>I can list impacts of weather and climate change on populations.</li></ul>	**Deep-Level Success Criteria for SEL** <ul><li>I can explain that resource distribution is not equitable in society.</li><li>I can analyze for meaning in the distributions of populations in a resource area.</li><li>I can deconstruct the causes behind resource distribution and populations.</li><li>I can draw conclusions about my environmental justice designation in contrast to other environmental justice populations.</li></ul>	**Transfer-Level Success Criteria for SEL** <ul><li>I can apply in a different context how populations are impacted differently in different environmental events, and what the outcomes are for each of those populations.</li><li>I can present to all people represented as environmental justice populations in a kind and considerate way.</li><li>I can present my data and analysis objectively to town or city planners and emergency services.</li></ul>

Figure 9.2: Example interdisciplinary SPBL unit plan.

continued ▶

Stage 3: Craft the driving question at the transfer level, adding authentic context for the unit.

Driving question: To what extent do varying experts predict the impact of sudden changes in the environment?

Authentic context: Students will simulate a professional work experience. What outside experts might you use?

According to the Environmental Protection Agency (EPA) (n.d.), *environmental justice* is the fair treatment and meaningful involvement of all people regardless of race, color, national origin, or income, with respect to the development, implementation, and enforcement of environmental laws, regulations, and policies.

This project will use that definition to have students identify and research local professionals that work with issues related to environmental justice. These professionals might include:

- Local FEMA representatives
- NOAA representatives
- Local police, fire, and ambulance services
- Town planners
- Local EPA or DCR representatives

Stage 4: Create tasks that align with the success criteria (specific strategies and activities).

Surface-Level Content Tasks	Deep-Level Content Tasks	Transfer-Level Content Tasks
Reading: Read excerpts from textbooks and other teacher-provided readings. **Writing:** Respond to predesignated prompts. Summarize basic text. **Speaking:** Present relevant information to a class. • Answer one, ask one • Charades • Kinesthetic mode (chalk walk through the heart)	**Reading:** Research relevant texts and databases. **Writing:** Summarize and contextualize readings. **Speaking:** Support a position or claim using evidence from text. • Predictions • Data collection • Four-square summary • Media productions (movie trailer, and so on) • Art rendering (watercolor succession, and so on) • Guest speakers • NEC Jeopardy	**Reading:** Find analogous texts, and relate them to the driving question for deeper context. **Writing:** Write a persuasive argument or essay using evidence and citations. **Speaking:** Debate and defend multiple viewpoints on an environmental issue. • Presentation to professionals • Debates • Research article summary • Equipment install project • Troubleshooting project
Surface-Level SEL Tasks	**Deep-Level SEL Tasks**	**Transfer-Level SEL Tasks**
Reading: I can identify problems about several communities, not just the ones I'm interested in. **Writing:** I can reflect on the predictions I have made to places that have had storm surge experiences in the past. **Speaking:** I can clearly present information summarizing my own predictions and the predictions of others in my group.	**Reading:** In a group, I can research and summarize global catastrophes and regional responses from the aspect of planning and equity. **Writing:** I can evaluate and explain past responses to inform future responses and policies. **Speaking:** I can make a convincing pitch about causes and effects and the impacts those have on specific communities, not just the ones in which I'm interested.	**Writing:** I can present evidence using resources from multiple disciplines and examples. **Speaking:** I can reflect through debate many points of view (within groups, between groups, and among institutions), defending the pros and cons of remediation efforts following a catastrophic event.

Stage 5: Create an entry event to launch the sustained-inquiry process.

Entry Event:

Students will watch several weather reports from storms and national emergencies. These will be set up like museum discovery stations in a walking gallery. They will form groups and try to identify what is missing from mainstream news reporting. Students will also watch segments from *Hurricane on the Bayou*, about the impact of Hurricane Katrina in Louisiana. Through a Socratic seminar, students will develop questions reflecting on the previous task and then debate the impacts of storm surges on local populations. Questions that should be teased from debate...

- What are they not hearing in the news?
- Do storms impact people or other things equally?
- Which communities/populations bear the brunt of a storm disaster?
- What will be the impact of storms as sea levels rise?
- How do emergency responders allocate funds and resources?

Source: © 2021 by Rose Young, Paul Crofts, and Richard Whitaker. Used with permission.
Source for standards: NGSS Lead States, 2013.

Allowing students to co-construct the success criteria and the driving question will increase clarity and student ownership in learning. Having teachers from different subject areas co-construct interdisciplinary SPBL units allows students to have increased opportunities for seeing how knowledge and skills from one subject area can transfer into another subject area.

Celebration

While it may feel like the reflect and refine stages of this step are purely about identifying areas for improvement, they will also reveal inevitable successes. Make sure you take the time to acknowledge these! In life, when you accomplish something challenging, you should always look for affirmations and celebrations. One cannot grow without change. Change in any context is challenging. Upon completion of the SPBL process, you should find ways to celebrate your success.

Richard DuFour, Rebecca DuFour, Robert Eaker, Thomas W. Many, and Mike Mattos (2016) emphasize: "When celebrations continually remind people of the purpose and priorities of their organizations, members are more likely to embrace the purpose and work toward agreed-on priorities" (p. 221). Effective celebrations "convince every staff member that he or she can be a winner and that his or her efforts can be noted and appreciated" (p. 223). DuFour and colleagues (2016) offer four keys for effectively incorporating celebrations into a school or district culture:

1. Explicitly state the purpose of the celebration.

2. Make celebration everyone's responsibility.

3. Establish a clear link between the recognition and the behavior or commitment you are attempting to encourage and reinforce.

4. Create opportunities to have many winners. (p. 223)

Celebrations should occur among students as well as members of your team. Take time to celebrate and self-affirm. It is essential! Following are a few ideas for student celebrations.

- Ask students prior to the end of the unit what an ideal and appropriate classroom celebration looks, sounds, and feels like (obviously, you must use some discretion here).

- Provide snacks.

- Provide some music.

- Have students participate in an affirmation activity (for example, they could write notes of affirmation to each other.

Teachers should use discretion when planning a classroom celebration, but it's important to celebrate. This is what we do as adults after we accomplish a large project or task. We should celebrate with students and affirm their hard work after they complete an SPBL unit.

Tips for Reflecting, Refining, and Celebrating

Following are some helpful tips for reflecting, refining, and celebrating.

- When it comes to reflection, focus on reflecting on what ways you did or did not meet your learning goal (step 3). Focus also on how well you implemented the teacher action research (step 4). Determine how well you answered the three SPBL questions.

- When it comes to refinement for students, after students complete the culminating public product and answer the driving question, ask students about how they might have answered the driving question differently. For example: "Excellent work! It was challenging work. You just answered an open-ended question and addressed an authentic problem. There is more than one correct answer to this question. Knowing what you know now, how might you answer it differently?"

- When it comes to refinement with your action research team, meet with team members and discuss ways not only to improve the SPBL unit you implemented but also challenge yourselves for the next unit. Consider integrating even more high-impact strategies, making it more authentic, or possibly showing students transfer by adding more interdisciplinary connections.

- When it comes to celebrations, it's hard for me to imagine something more rewarding as a teacher or student than completing an authentic and rigorous learning challenge, such as that presented in an SPBL unit. In life, when we collectively work hard and accomplish something great, we should take the time to celebrate the things worth celebrating. Part of sustaining something great is honoring the experience through celebration.

Summary

This chapter provided clear guidance on the final step of the SPBL process: reflect, refine, and celebrate. It is imperative that both students and teachers reflect on what they learned from the unit and whether they met the learning intentions. As a team, there are several ways you might push yourselves to increase learning for students as well as empower them to have even more ownership over their learning. Though the five steps are helpful and show a clear *how*, always make the SPBL process about the integrity to the learner and the evidence of the learning taking place.

Questions for Reflection

Individually or in collaborative teams, answer the following questions to reflect on your learning in this chapter.

1. What is the difference between reflecting and refining?

2. Reflecting on how you and your team structured your assessments, what is something you want to refine?

3. How will you celebrate with your students and your team?

Challenge

Once you have implemented your SPBL unit, even if it did not go exactly the way you had hoped, commit to refining the process. What ways can your lean into gathering constructive feedback from both students and your team to make the next SPBL process even better?

CHAPTER 10

TRANSFERRING LEARNING THROUGH THREE SIMULTANEOUS EXPERIENCES

The SPBL process is inspired by specific questions I have heard from various groups of educators. I was inspired by educators with PBL backgrounds, educators with a background in professional learning communities (PLCs), and educators who had a genuine passion for social and emotional learning. I heard these questions over the course of twenty years in education both from colleagues in my school and in schools I visited as a consultant across the United States. These questions include:

- "PBL takes too long to plan and implement. How is it sustainable?"

- "How do we ensure students are learning content at deep and transfer levels?"

Educators who have a background in organizing teacher collaboration time come to this work with the following questions.

- "How do we use teacher collaboration time more efficiently and effectively so we focus on the evidence of student learning?"

- "How might we use protocols to analyze not only standardized test data but also the quality of student work?"

Educators who have a passion for and background in social and emotional learning come to this work with the following questions.

- "How should we best structure and discuss our formative assessments?"

- "How should we define and assess SEL?"

- "How might SEL be genuinely integrated into the curriculum and not siloed as a separate initiative?"

- "How do we place a high value on SEL while still maintaining a focus on academic content?"

The intent of this book is to answer those questions with one comprehensive but practical process. The SPBL process involves planning SPBL units and assessments, establishing clear goals for learning, implementing in action research, and engaging in reflection. SPBL is a process that asks us, as educators, to model being learners with and for our students.

Previously in the book, I discussed the scene from *The Karate Kid* (Weintraub & Avildsen, 1984) when Mr. Miyagi's student Daniel LaRusso gets frustrated because he does not see the point of having to do all the chores around Mr. Miyagi's house. Daniel does not see that Mr. Miyagi is teaching for transfer. The skills and strengths Daniel gains while doing these chores allow him to transfer those skills to a different context, karate. In this final chapter, I will unpack the three experiences that are hopefully taking place simultaneously during the SPBL process: (1) the student experience, (2) the teacher team experience, and (3) the individual educator experience.

The Student Experience

The SPBL process promotes student growth not only in content knowledge and understanding but also in social and emotional skills. During this process, students should become more capable of self-assessment. Students should be able to identify where they are in their learning. Students should be thinking things such as, "As I think about the driving question and what I have learned so far, I am currently at the deep level of my learning because I can compare and contrast the Southern economy and the Northern economy during the 1850s. I am not quite at the transfer level yet because I am not sure of the extent to which I can apply this information to help abolish slavery today."

The SPBL process should establish the opportunity for students to do the following.

- Learn at the surface, deep, and transfer levels.
- Grow in content knowledge as well as SEL skills.
- Become capable of self-assessment.
- Understand how they can apply and utilize the work they produce in a real-world context.
- Experience learning that promotes equity.

The SPBL process provides students with a meaningful and valuable learning experience. The most significant outcome of this process is the student experience.

The Teacher Team Experience

As students work on their SPBL unit, teachers work on their own SPBL unit. The entry event for teachers might be reading this book or attending professional development focused on this work. The culminating public product for teachers is the actual implementation of the unit. The audience is the students. Students have milestones throughout the unit that indicate their progress in learning and toward the culminating public product. Likewise, teachers have milestones, planning templates, and protocols to analyze qualitative and quantitative student work, and instruction to adapt based on the data. The ideal SPBL process establishes the opportunity for teacher teams to do the following.

- Grow in collective efficacy.
- Experience team meetings grounded in vulnerability-based trust and equal input.
- Make instructional decisions based on qualitative and quantitative student data.
- Have autonomy and ownership in what is taught and what is learned.
- Grow in clarity around learning intentions and success criteria.

The SPBL process provides teacher teams with a chance to engage in conversations about learning at the surface, deep, and transfer levels. It is grounded in setting goals, conducting action research, and adjusting instruction to grow students' SEL skills and content knowledge. Without a quality teacher action research team, it's much more difficult for PBL to be sustainable.

The Individual Experience

The final experience, the one that may not be as obvious, is personal growth for individual educators going through this process. This experience is for the individual educator, the individual teacher, the individual administrator, or the individual counselor.

There is a reason why airlines ask parents to first put on their oxygen masks before helping their children. We are no good to students if we do not first take care of ourselves. Throughout the book, I have primarily talked about the student experience and the teacher team experience. Now, let's change the context. Let's now look through the lens of the individual educator experience, at each of us individually. Figure 10.1 shows how individual teachers can use the three SPBL questions for reflection.

SPBL Questions	Individual Educator Reflections
1. How do you ensure at least one year's growth in one year's time (for yourself)?	The best learners are the best teachers. Teachers should model being learners for students. How are you modeling your commitment to growing professionally or growing personally, outside the context of school? The individual teacher should be committed to growing every year and modeling learning for and with their students.
2. How do you ensure an equal intensity of surface-, deep-, and transfer-level learning for each unit of study?	As you think about your own individual growth in learning, to what extent are you genuinely learning something new and applying it? Are you not only learning new things, but also applying them?
3. How do you define and provide intentional feedback (self-reflection) to yourself in necessary skills such as responsible decision making, self-awareness, social awareness, self-management, and relationship skills?	How are you taking it upon yourself to grow in your awareness of responsible decision making, self-awareness, social awareness, self-management, and relationship skills?

Figure 10.1: Three SPBL questions for individual teacher reflection.

The SPBL process is intended to promote self-reflection and personal growth. The three questions apply to you not only in a professional context but also in a personal context. Consider the educators and other people who have made the most significant impact on your life. To what extent were they committed to the following three things?

1. Continuous growth

2. Transfer-level teaching and learning (learning that is authentic and empowering)

3. Growth in self-awareness, responsible decision making, self-management, social awareness, and relationship skills

Those qualities are what we want from the ideal graduate. Those are what we want from colleagues, and those are what we want for ourselves.

Summary

SPBL is really three experiences in one process. The first is the student experience. Students will engage in a learning experience that has an equal intensity of surface, deep, and transfer levels of learning. Students will grow in their self-assessment capability. They will grow in content knowledge as well as explicitly clear SEL competencies. The second experience is the teacher team's experience with action research. The team will generate a SMART goal around both a content learning intention and an SEL learning intention. The goal involves analyzing both qualitative and quantitative data and determining clear next steps based on outcomes of the analysis. The goal also commits the team to the protocols it will use during the action research. The third and final experience is focused on the personal growth of the individual teacher. As individuals, educators should challenge themselves to effectively answer the three SPBL questions, simply changing the context of the questions to make them personal.

Questions for Reflection

Individually or in collaborative teams, answer the following questions to reflect on your learning in this chapter.

1. Which of the three experiences of the SPBL process will be the most challenging for you? Why?

2. In what ways can the SPBL process promote meaningful and authentic learning for *all* students?

3. If you are hesitant about implementing the SPBL process, what is holding you back? Why?

Challenge

Make a commitment with a trusted colleague or team of colleagues to implement at least two SPBL units throughout the year. Track your goal data, and compare the evidence of learning to a unit you and your team taught in a more traditional fashion. Start with one unit, and implement the SPBL process.

APPENDIX A:
GLOSSARY OF KEY TERMS

authenticity. The PBL design element that means the unit has a real-world context; uses real-world processes, tools, and quality standards; makes a real impact; and is connected to students' concerns, interests, and identities. (PBLWorks, 2021).

CASEL. An acronym for Collaborative for Academic, Social, and Emotional Learning. The five CASEL competencies that help define SEL include (1) self-awareness, (2) social awareness, (3) responsible decision making, (4) self-management, and (5) relationship skills (CASEL, n.d.b).

critique and revision. The PBL design element that involves the process of giving and receiving feedback in order to revise ideas and products or conduct further inquiry (PBLWorks, 2021).

culminating public product. The PBL design element that involves the means for how students demonstrate what they learn (for example, an artifact, a presentation, a performance, or an event) and can share with people beyond the classroom. Students make their project work public by sharing it with and explaining or presenting it to people beyond the classroom (PBLWorks, 2021).

deep learning. The ability to make connections, compare and contrast, establish cause and effect, and answer why.

driving question. The one overarching question in an SPBL unit that restates the learning intention and poses a problem or challenge. The need-to-knows that students generate as a result of a driving question can function as effective indicators of the question's level of quality.

effect size. A simple way of quantifying the difference between two groups. The formula for effect size is: effect size = mean of experimental group – mean of control group (standard deviation; Hattie, 2009).

entry document. The document, often in the form of a letter, given to students to introduce a PBL unit and begin the entry event. The document states the driving question or challenge, incorporates key expectations for the unit, and might include outside experts who can be utilized during the process. The document is used as a reference to help students maintain focus and clarity throughout the process.

entry event. The thoughtful hook that kicks off an SPBL unit. Teachers can implement entry events in a variety of formats, including displaying pictures, showing a video clip, incorporating staggering statistics, and taking their class on a field trip. An entry event incorporates the driving question and possibly an entry document. Sometimes an outside expert can be used as part of the entry event.

formative assessment. Any assessment that is *for* learning; any formal or informal check for student understanding that teachers can use to alter or adjust their instruction. Within the context of an SPBL unit, formative assessments are in the form of both quantitative measurements, such as multiple-choice tests that measure student growth in surface and deep learning, and qualitative measurements, such as key milestones that measure growth toward the answer to the driving question and culminating public product.

learning intention. A brief statement that describes what the student should know and be able to do. Learning intentions are major concepts from the content that justify an entire unit of study (for example, historical research, the quadratic equation, and persuasive writing). Learning intentions are void of context.

milestone. A major event, building block, or formative assessment within the context of a PBL unit of study. Milestones are essential in the PBL process to check for understanding as well as help drive the sustained-inquiry process. Milestones should progress from surface to deep to transfer levels of learning.

minilesson. Whole-group instruction (often teacher-led direct instruction) conducted with a conscious effort to build background knowledge in an efficient amount of time.

need-to-know. A student-generated question that goes to the heart of the learning intention. Student need-to-knows are integral to the sustained-inquiry process.

project-based learning (PBL). "A teaching method in which students gain knowledge and skills by working for an extended period of time to investigate and respond to an authentic, engaging, and complex question, problem, or challenge" (PBLWorks, n.d.).

protocol. A structured multistep process that allows participants (students and teachers) in the process an equal opportunity to be engaged. A protocol promotes honest and efficient feedback and is often used to analyze student work.

reflection. The process of thinking about one's learning, the effectiveness of one's inquiry and project activities, the quality of work, and obstacles that arise and strategies for overcoming them (PBLWorks, 2021).

rigor. An equal intensity of surface-, deep-, and transfer-level learning within the context of a unit of study (McDowell, 2021).

scaffold. The strategies used to ensure each individual student has support for meeting the surface-, deep-, and transfer-level success criteria Examples of scaffolds include whole-group, small-group, or individual instruction; a note-taking guide; and an adjustment made to an activity or protocol. The hope is the scaffold can eventually be removed and students can meet the success criteria with fewer or no scaffolds in place.

social and emotional learning (SEL). For the purpose of this book, the five SEL competencies determined by CASEL (n.d.b): (1) self-awareness, (2) social awareness, (3) responsible decision making, (4) self-management, and (5) relationship skills.

success criteria. Specific learning targets that state what students must demonstrate at the surface, deep, and transfer levels of learning to meet the learning intention (McDowell, 2017).

summative assessment. An assessment that is *of* learning. It represents the culmination of what students know and understand at the end of a unit of study or course. A final exam or unit test and a culminating public product are examples of summative assessments. In the SPBL process, students typically have two summative assessments for each unit of study. One is a culminating public product, and another is a more traditional assessment that can help determine growth at the surface, deep, and transfer levels of learning.

surface learning. Basic knowledge of the facts of a major concept.

sustainable project-based learning (SPBL). A process in which there is equal commitment to:

- Using the PBL design elements as an instructional framework for planning and implementing units of study

- Clearly identifying and assessing both key academic concepts and social and emotional concepts

- Regularly meeting in teacher teams using protocols for action research, and discussing the three SPBL questions (CASEL, n.d.b).

1. How do you ensure at least one year's growth in one year's time?

2. How do you ensure an equal intensity of surface-, deep-, and transfer-level learning for each unit of study?

3. How do you define and provide intentional feedback to students on their growth in both content knowledge and SEL skills?

sustained inquiry. The PBL design element that involves a consistent process of student-generated questions (or need-to-knows) that drive the teaching and learning taking place. These questions go to the heart of the learning intentions.

transfer learning. The ability to apply content knowledge and skills in a new or different context. In SPBL, the goal is that students can apply surface- and deep-level knowledge in one or multiple real-world contexts.

voice and choice. A PBL design element in which students have significant ownership in determining their goals, challenges, solutions, and products. Student work is centered on a clear learning intention and success criteria.

APPENDIX B:
PROTOCOL LIBRARY

What? So What? Now What? Protocol

This protocol allows you to connect to others and examine their work, while simultaneously allowing all group members to get useful feedback.

	What the Presenter Does	What the Audience Does	Time Allotted
What?	Explains the quantitative or qualitative data Explains the learning intention and success criteria What level of learning do you feel it represents (surface, deep, or transfer) and why?	Listens and takes notes using sentence stems like the following: • I liked . . . • I wonder . . . • I suggest . . . • Questions this raises for me in my own work include . . .	Four minutes
So What?	Sits down, listens, and takes notes on audience feedback	Verbally shares notes generated in the What?, using the same sentence stems: • I liked . . . • I wonder . . . • I suggest . . . • Questions this raises for me in my own work include . . .	Four minutes
Now What?	Explains how the feedback resonated and what next steps might be	Listens	Three minutes
Total time:			Eleven minutes

Source: Adapted from Thompson-Grove, G. (2017). What? So what? Now what? *Accessed at www.schoolreforminitiative.org /download /what-so-what-now-what on December 10, 2021.*

Examining Student Work Protocol

This protocol allows you to provide honest and efficient constructive feedback on student work.

Setup: 1. Review the protocol. 2. Determine the facilitator and timekeeper.	Two minutes
Presenter: The presenter takes the following actions. 1. Presents the project context and driving question 2. Describes the teaching and learning context, standards, and learning intentions 3. Describes how the essential PBL elements were incorporated into the project 4. Describes the best teaching practices and protocols used throughout the project 5. Shares materials related to learning and student work (likely a milestone from the unit) 6. Poses one or two focus questions about the teaching and learning that took place for which the presenter specifically wants feedback	Ten minutes
Clarifying Questions by Participants: Participants ask nonevaluative questions about the project using the language of the learning intention and success criteria.	Three minutes
Individual Silent Writing: Participants review notes about the presentation and record thoughts on how to address the focus questions. • What did the students do well? • What evidence exists in the work samples to support this?	Three minutes
Participant Discussion While the Presenter Takes Notes: The presenter remains silent while participants provide feedback using the following sentence stems (round-robin style): • Round 1: "I noticed . . ." or "I observed . . ." • Round 2: "I wonder . . ." • Round 3: "In the future, consider . . ."	Nine minutes
Debriefing: The presenter discusses the feedback and identifies areas of success and challenge within the unit.	Three minutes
Total time:	Thirty minutes

Source: Adapted from Baron, D. (2017). Examining student work: A constructivist protocol. Accessed at www.nsrfharmony.org /wp-content/uploads/2017/10/constructivist_student.pdf on December 10, 2021.

Tuning Protocol

You can use this protocol for a peer critique (students) or to critique a variety of documents (teachers), such as the completed SPBL planning template, SPBL culminating public product rubric, SPBL formative assessment map, or SPBL anticipated need-to-know map.

Presentation	Presenter presents qualitative or quantitative evidence of learning.	Five minutes
Clarification	Audience asks a clarifying question (for example, "Can you please repeat the learning intention?").	One minute
I Liked Statements	Presenter listens (even turns around so their back is to the audience) and takes notes. Audience discusses specific aspects of the artifact and presentation they like.	Three minutes
I Wonder Statements	Presenter listens (remains turned around if comfortable) and continues to take notes. Audience discusses possible areas of development.	Three minutes
Possible Next Steps	Presenter listens (remains turned around if comfortable) and continues to take notes. Audience discusses specific suggested next steps.	Three minutes
Reflection	Presenter turns around and discusses what feedback they found helpful.	Three minutes
Open Discussion	Presenter and audience members have an open discussion sharing additional ideas and resources.	Two minutes
Total time:		Twenty minutes

Source: Adapted from School Reform Initiative. (2017c). Tuning protocol guidelines. *Accessed at www.schoolreforminitiative.org/download/tuning-protocol-guidelines on January 27, 2022.*

Lesson Study Protocol

You can use this protocol to conduct observable action research in which you co-plan and then observe aspects of the SPBL unit in another classroom.

SMART Goal Connection	The team determines specific success criteria or learning outcome they want to focus on as it relates to the predetermined learning goal (or SMART goal) from step 3 of the SPBL process.	Ten minutes
Co-Planning	The team members co-plan a specific lesson or strategy based on a clear learning intention and success criteria (for either content, SEL, or both).	Forty-five to sixty minutes
Observation	One team member volunteers to implement the lesson while other team members observe. The observers take intentional notes using sentence stems such as: • I liked . . . • I wonder . . . • I suggest . . .	Fifteen to twenty minutes
Debriefing	Team members reconvene, discuss the feedback, and determine next steps for other team members to implement. The team should consider using John Hattie's research (Hattie's influences from Visible Learningmeta^X.com) to locate high-impact strategies and determine how and where they fit within the context of an SPBL unit.	Twenty minutes
Total time:		110 to 130 minutes

Source: Adapted from Doig, B., & Groves, S. (2011). Japanese lesson study: Teacher professional development through communities of inquiry. Mathematics Teacher Education and Development, 13*(1), 77–93.*

Focused Observation Protocol

Similar to the Lesson Study Protocol, you and your team can use this protocol to conduct a teacher-to-teacher observation regarding something related to the learning goal from step 3.

Observed	The team member being observed asks for specific feedback on success criteria or the impact of a strategy. Ideally, this is directly tied to the team's SMART goal.	Five minutes (Can be done well in advance of the actual focused observation.)
Observer	This could be all the other team members or just one other team member. Observers take notes using sentence stems (such as *I like . . .*, *I wonder . . .*, or *Next steps might be . . .*). These notes should focus on the specific success criteria or strategy the observed teacher requested.	Fifteen to twenty minutes
Total time:		Twenty to twenty-five minutes

Source: Adapted from School Reform Initiative. (2017b). Peer coaching: Observer as coach. *Accessed at www.schoolreform initiative.org/download/peer-coaching-observer-as-coach on January 23, 2022.*

Charrette Protocol

This is a much shorter version of the Tuning Protocol. You can use this protocol for a peer critique (students) or to critique a variety of documents (teachers), such as the completed SPBL planning template, SPBL culminating public product rubric, SPBL formative assessment map, or SPBL anticipated need-to-know map.

Presenter Speech	Presenter shares evidence of student learning at each level of learning (surface, deep, and transfer). Presenter says something they feel insecure about and want feedback on regarding the milestone (or quantitative data or planning document).	Three minutes
Clarification	Partner asks clarifying questions (for example, "Could you please repeat what you said about . . . ?").	One minute
Feedback	Partner gives suggestions focusing on the specific thing the presenter wanted feedback on. Feedback is kind, helpful, and specific. • "I like . . ." • "I wonder . . ." Presenter takes notes and remains silent.	Three minutes
Discussion	Partner engages in open discussion. How was this feedback helpful?	Three minutes
Total time:		Ten minutes (This time represents one round.)

Source: Adapted from School Reform Initiative. (2017a). The Charrette protocol. Accessed at www.schoolreforminitiative.org /download/charrette-protocol on January 27, 2022.

Inter-Rater Reliability Protocol

The purpose of this protocol is to help the teacher action research team develop inner-rater reliability for their qualitative common assessments or milestones.

Prework	Team members determine what example of student work they want to focus on. This should be based on a common formative assessment pre-established in the SMART goal. The team should have a common standards-based rubric that clearly defines the success criteria for surface, deep, and transfer levels of learning. Team members bring one sample of each category (exemplary, proficient, and progressing) of the student work to the team meeting, hiding student names.	
Randomization	With no student names, team members mix up all the student work samples and hand each team member three samples (again, the samples are random).	Two minutes
Analysis	Team members study the rubric and determine the rank or category (exemplary, proficient, or progressing) for each of the three student work samples.	Five minutes
Reaching of Consensus	Team members openly discuss their rankings and reach consensus on what exemplary, proficient, and progressing samples look like.	Five minutes
Exemplary Discussion	The team answers and discusses the question, "Based on the success criteria in the rubric, why were certain students successful, and how might we challenge their learning?"	Five minutes
Proficient Discussion	The team answers and discusses the question, "Based on the success criteria in the rubric, why did certain students perform at the proficient level, what did they struggle with, and what actions might we take to get them to exemplary?"	Five minutes
Progressing Discussion	The team answers and discusses the question, "Based on the success criteria in the rubric, why did certain students struggle, what did they struggle with, and what actions might we take?"	Five minutes
Next Steps	The team summarizes and is clear on the next steps for implementing interventions and high-yield strategies. The team should consider strategies that have a high effect size.	Five minutes
Connection to SMART Goal	The team discusses connections to its SMART goal and the three SPBL questions.	Five minutes
Total time:		Thirty-seven minutes

Harkness Discussion Protocol

The purpose of this protocol is to promote discussion. Students can use this protocol during class, or the teacher action research team can use it during a team meeting. This protocol encourages all members to participate equitably in a discussion.

Look at the Student Work Sample	Do a close analysis on a qualitative or quantitative student work sample. The purpose of the analysis is to address one or all three of the following question 1. How does this artifact demonstrate student academic growth? 2. What evidence of student learning do you have for surface-, deep-, and transfer-level learning within the context of each unit of study? 3. How does this demonstrate understanding of the designated SEL skill?	Ten minutes
Discuss	Place chairs in a circle to conduct a group discussion. During the discussion: • Focus on what is within your control (Avoid tangents on factors outside your control.) • Use the three-then-me technique (After you contribute to the discussion, give at least three people an opportunity to contribute before you contribute again.) • Help create an environment where everyone feels comfortable contributing • Discuss one or all three questions • Have the facilitator (or designee) draw a line each time someone speaks (The goal is that by the end of the discussion, the drawing should look like a web.)	Fifteen minutes
Total time:		Twenty-five minutes

Source: Adapted from Courchesne, C. G. (2005, Spring). "A suggestion of a fundamental nature": Imagining a legal education of solely electives taught as discussions. Rutgers Law Record, 29(21), 21–63.

Gallery Walk Protocol

The purpose of this protocol is to provide constructive feedback on evidence of work. Students can use this protocol in class for peer feedback, or the teacher action research team can use it for critiquing a variety of documents, such as the completed SPBL planning template, SPBL culminating public product rubric, SPBL formative assessment map, or SPBL anticipated need-to-know map.

Framing	Post large butcher or poster paper. Format the posters to include all the criteria on which you want feedback. When doing this with multiple people, design a template for consistency in formatting.	Two minutes
Feedback Frames	During the feedback session, participants silently walk around the room to each poster. They write feedback (praise or polish statements) on small sticky notes and stick them on the individual posters. Use the following sentence stems for feedback: • **Praise:** "I noticed that . . ." • **Polish:** "You might consider . . ." 1. The learning intention states the goal of learning, and it is free of context. 2. The success criteria provide ingredients for meeting the learning intention. 3. The driving question provides context, provides a *why*, and restates the learning intention. 4. The tasks allow students to show evidence of learning at each level (surface, deep, and transfer).	Fifteen minutes
Reflection	Participants reflect on their experience with the protocol using stems such as *Now, I feel . . .* and *Before, I felt . . .*	Five minutes
Total time:		Twenty-two minutes

Goal-Setting Protocol

The purpose of this protocol is to help the teacher action research team determine the learning goal (SPBL process, step 3). This protocol can be helpful if the team is having difficulty coming up with an idea for a good student learning goal or building consensus on what the goal should be.

Individually, review the data sets: What stands out? What is affirming? What is surprising?	Ten minutes
With a partner, review the data sets: What themes should you focus on to craft your goals?	Ten minutes
With four team members, share your goal idea. Come to consensus on what you think one goal should be.	Twenty minutes
Individually, evaluate one goal using the following questions. • Is it strategic and specific? • Is it measurable? • Is it attainable? • Is it results oriented? • Is it time bound? If a goal is not SMART (Conzemius & O'Neill, 2014), rewrite it so it is.	Five minutes
With your team, prepare a presentation of your goal.	Ten minutes
With your team, present your SMART goal (five minutes for each presentation), answering the following questions. • How did you come up with your goal? • What were the challenges around reaching consensus? • Why is your goal the most important thing to focus on? • How is your goal SMART?	Ten minutes
Engage in open sharing, with everyone discussing what they like, their questions, and their suggestions.	Five minutes
Conclude with an open discussion about which goals are the best fit for your team.	Eight minutes
Total time:	Seventy-eight minutes (Adjust times as needed.)

Source: Conzemius, A. E., & O'Neill, J. (2014). The handbook for SMART school teams: Revitalizing best practices for collaboration (2nd ed.). Bloomington, IN: Solution Tree Press; adapted from Davis, J. (2021). Goal setting protocol. Accessed at www.schoolreforminitiative.org/download/goal-setting-protocol on January 23, 2022.

APPENDIX C:
EXAMPLE SPBL UNIT PLANS

Example 1: Grade 8 Mathematics

SPBL Unit Plan

Stage 1: Learning Intentions (a Major Concept for the Unit and a CASEL Competency)
1. Content learning intention: I can apply the knowledge gained from learning about linear equations and systems of linear equations in order to make an informed decision on which mortgage would be the best decision for different scenarios (PS.1, PS.2, PS.3, PS.4, PS.5, PS.6, PS.7, PS.8, AI.DS.3, AI.L.3, AI.L.4, AI.L.5, AI.L.6, AI.SEI.1, AI.SEI.3, AI.SEI.4). **2. SEL learning intention (responsible decision making):** I can make an informed financial decision for purchasing a house using a mortgage based on multiple different variables, including but not limited to income, other expenses, roommate situation, down payments, and interest rates.

Stage 2: Success Criteria (Daily Learning Goals)
You could have multiple goals, written without context or specificity.

Surface-Level Success Criteria for Content	**Deep-Level Success Criteria for Content**	**Transfer-Level Success Criteria for Content**
• I can write the equation of a line given the slope and *y*-intercept. • I can write the equation of a line given two coordinate points. • I can find the intersection of two lines through graphing, substitution, or elimination.	• I can interpret the slope and *y*-intercept of a line given a real-world context. • I can translate a real-world situation into a mathematics problem. • I can interpret the intersection of two lines, as well as the initial and ending behavior of two lines, given a real-world context.	I can use my knowledge of the way linear equations work to make an informed financial decision for purchasing a house using a mortgage based on the criteria presented to me.
Surface-Level Success Criteria for SEL	**Deep-Level Success Criteria for SEL**	**Transfer-Level Success Criteria for SEL**
I can define various terms, including, but not limited to, *financial literacy, mortgage, interest rate, down payment, income, expenses,* and *break-even point.*	I can explain the impact that changing variables, such as interest rate, down payment, length of mortgage, and others, will have on both immediate and long-term financial situations and goals.	I can use my knowledge of the way linear equations work to make an informed financial decision for purchasing a house using a mortgage based on the criteria presented to me.

Stage 3: Driving Question (Written at the Transfer Level)

Driving question: To what extent can we use mathematics in order to create a more financially literate world?

Authentic context: Students will simulate being loan officers for a mortgage company, giving advice to people seeking to purchase a home. "Judges" will be given various scenarios or situations in order to seek advice from the loan officers.

Stage 4: Tasks (Specific Strategies and Activities)

Surface-Level Content Tasks	Deep-Level Content Tasks	Transfer-Level Content Tasks
Reading: Engage in minilessons on slope, *y*-intercepts, linear equations, and systems of linear equations. **Writing:** Do practice assignments on writing, graphing, and solving linear equations, as well as systems of linear equations. **Speaking:** Do a 2-1-1 with two classmates on what methods you prefer to write, solve, and graph linear equations or systems of linear equations.	**Reading:** Read multiple real-world contexts that can be represented using linear equations. **Writing:** Write your own interpretations of slope, *y*-intercept, intersection of lines, and the beginning and ending behavior of the lines that represent your real-world context. **Speaking:** Do a think-pair-share to brainstorm how this might help you apply your knowledge to the entire project.	**Reading:** Consider the scenario presented to you that provides you with multiple different variables. **Writing:** Use the variables to find a house that you want to purchase. Then, write multiple equations that represent different options for purchasing that house using a mortgage. Create some graphic organizers to model your equations. **Speaking:** Explain the real-world meaning of each part of each equation that you wrote to the "judge."
Surface-Level SEL Tasks	**Deep-Level SEL Tasks**	**Transfer-Level SEL Tasks**
Reading: Read articles that discuss issues in financial literacy. **Writing:** Complete a worksheet on definitions of financial literacy terms. **Speaking:** Have small-group discussions on the importance and impact of financial literacy.	**Reading:** Read articles about policy in poverty and science in poverty. **Writing:** Write a reflection on your individual belief for the driving force of financial illiteracy. **Speaking:** Debate whether science and mathematics or policy is more influential in helping combat financial illiteracy.	**Reading:** Read a family scenario that gives in-depth detail about the home the family is looking to buy, as well as other factors (such as income). **Writing:** Write and graph multiple equations that represent multiple mortgage options for the same house. **Speaking:** Present the family's options, and suggest which option you would choose as well as why you believe the family should choose that option.

Stage 5: Entry Event
A loan officer will come in and explain the basics of what he or she does as a job—"a day in the life of a loan officer." He or she will describe the basics of a mortgage and why helping the customer select the correct mortgage is important. Students will use a "know or need-to-know" format to begin the process of inquiry. Know or need-to-know categories will be: • Mortgages • Linear equations • Systems of linear equations

Source: © 2021 by Joel Haynie. Used with permission.
Source for standards: Indiana Department of Education. (2019a). Indiana academic standards, mathematics: Algebra I. *Indianapolis, IN: Author. Accessed at www.doe.in.gov/sites/default/files/standards/algebra-i-standards-dec-2020.pdf on October 7, 2021; Indiana Department of Education. (2020b).* Indiana academic standards, mathematics: Grade 8. *Indianapolis, IN: Author. Accessed at www.doe.in.gov/sites/default/files/standards/grade8-math-standards-dec-2020.pdf on October 7, 2021.*

Example 2: Grade 9 Biology for English Learners

SPBL Unit Plan

Stage 1: Learning Intentions (a Major Concept for the Unit and a CASEL Competency)

1. Content learning intention: I can apply my understanding of ecosystem dynamics to create a proposal for the protection and conservation of an endangered species (HS-LS1-5.6.7, HS-LS2-1–8, HS-LS4-5.6).

2. Language learning intention: I can use objective and evaluative language to construct an evidence-based scientific solution (ELD-SC.9.12).

3. SEL learning intention (responsible decision making): I can consider how my personal behavior impacts the environment and demonstrate an ability to make caring and constructive choices for the well-being of Earth's inhabitants.

Stage 2: Success Criteria (Daily Learning Goals)

You could have multiple goals, written without context or specificity.

Surface-Level Success Criteria for Content	Deep-Level Success Criteria for Content	Transfer-Level Success Criteria for Content
I can define key terms such as *ecology, ecosystem, trophic cascade, limiting factor, endangered,* and *biodiversity.*	I can explain how human activities disrupt the flow of energy or the cycling of matter in ecosystems.	I can apply my knowledge of ecological principles to current anthropogenic environmental issues.
Surface-Level Success Criteria for Language	**Deep-Level Success Criteria for Language**	**Transfer-Level Success Criteria for Language**
I can paraphrase the central ideas of multiple sources using a variety of linguistic structures.	I can use clauses to link claims with evidence and reasoning.	I can ask and answer questions to theorize, clarify, and refine solutions.
Surface-Level Success Criteria for SEL	**Deep-Level Success Criteria for SEL**	**Transfer-Level Success Criteria for SEL**
I can describe how human activities impact Earth's environment.	I can evaluate my role in environmental problems.	I can present personal solutions to collective environmental problems.

Stage 3: Driving Question (Written at the Transfer Level)

Driving question: To what extent can we reduce our impact on the environment?

Authentic context: Students will investigate the components of a healthy ecosystem and evaluate how their own actions affect the environment. Acting as environmental scientists, students will propose a research-based personal solution to a collective environmental issue.

Stage 4: Tasks (Specific Strategies and Activities)

Surface-Level Content Tasks	Deep-Level Content Tasks	Transfer-Level Content Tasks
Reading: Summarize key ideas about Earth's biodiversity using infographics. English learner (EL) support: Modeling **Writing:** Organize feeding relationships for an ecosystem into a food web. EL support: Native language partner **Speaking:** Introduce an endangered species to the class. EL support: Sentence starters	**Reading:** Analyze the role of humans in trophic cascades using an article. EL support: Reciprocal teaching **Writing:** Compare and contrast the characteristics of endangered species. EL support: Report frame **Speaking:** Prioritize the conservation efforts for several endangered species. EL support: Talk-moves sentence stems	**Reading:** Research the effects of human activities on Earth's biomes. EL support: Graphic organizer **Writing:** Write a persuasive letter lobbying for protection of an endangered species. EL support: Writing checklist **Speaking:** Present a zoo exhibit proposal for an endangered species to a target audience. EL support: *Who, what, when, where, why,* and *how* prompts
Surface-Level SEL Tasks	**Deep-Level SEL Tasks**	**Transfer-Level SEL Tasks**
Reading: Read the poem "Earthrise" by Amanda Gorman (Sierra Club, 2021). EL support: Video of the poem read aloud (Climate Reality, 2018) **Writing:** Create a concept map showing connections between personal activities and global environmental issues. EL support: Word bank **Speaking:** Discuss the value of biodiversity and healthy ecosystems in small groups. EL support: Labeled diagram	**Reading:** Read short profiles about teenage environmental activists. EL support: Graphic organizer **Writing:** Reflect on a personal ecological footprint calculation. EL support: Optional writing prompts **Speaking:** Engage in World Café conversations on the Power of One philosophy of change. EL support: Talk-moves sentence stems	**Reading:** Review peer proposals and provide feedback focused on human impacts and conservation solutions. EL support: Peer feedback checklist **Writing:** Focus on connecting protection and conservation of an endangered species to the collective well-being of Earth's environment and inhabitants. EL support: Collaborative concept map **Speaking:** Present a proposal with a focus on a personal solution to a collective environmental issue. EL support: *Who, what, when, where, why,* and *how* notecards

Stage 5: Entry Event

Students will participate in a field trip to the local zoo. Students will make observations and read signage regarding the recurring themes of the unit: biodiversity, human impacts, and conservation. Students will record thoughts, patterns, and details about the animals at the zoo using a one-page organizer. Following the field trip, students will choose one endangered species to focus on throughout the unit.

Source: © *2021 by Kara House. Used with permission; Climate Reality. (2018, December 4).* 24 hours of reality: "Earthrise" by Amanda Gorman *[Video]. Accessed at www.youtube.com/watch?v=xwOvBv8RLmo on October 8, 2021; Sierra Club. (2021).* Earthrise poem by Amanda Gorman. *Accessed at www.sierraclub.org/los-padres/blog/2021/02/earthrise-poem-amanda-gorman on January 10, 2022.*

Source for standards: Indiana Department of Education. (2016). Biology science standards. *Indianapolis, IN: Author. Accessed at www.in.gov/doe/files/indiana-biology-standards-2016-41116.pdf on October 7, 2021; WIDA. (2020).* WIDA English language development standards framework, 2020 edition: Kindergarten–grade 12. *Accessed at https://wida.wisc.edu/sites /default/files/resource/WIDA-ELD-Standards-Framework-2020-Edition-Grades-9-12.pdf on October 7, 2021.*

Example 3: Grades 10–12 Algebra II

SPBL Unit Plan
Stage 1: Learning Intentions (a Major Concept for the Unit and a CASEL Competency)

1. Content learning intention: I can apply mathematical skills of logarithmic and exponential functions to model an infectious disease (AII.CNE.1–6; AII.F.1–5; AII.SE.1–3; AII.Q.1–3; AII.EL.1–7; AII.PR.1–3; AII.DSP.1–6).

2. SEL learning intention (responsible decision making): I can use the mathematics of logarithms and exponentials to model a disease outbreak to assist the health department in making informed decisions as well as planning for such an event.

Stage 2: Success Criteria (Daily Learning Goals)

You could have multiple goals, written without context or specificity.

Surface-Level Success Criteria for Content	**Deep-Level Success Criteria for Content**	**Transfer-Level Success Criteria for Content**
• I can identify graphs as representing either exponential growth or decay. • I can identify the key elements of an exponential function and a logarithmic function. • I can use the properties or definition of logarithms to manipulate expressions and solve basic equations.	• I can apply exponential growth and decay models to basic real-world situations. • I can make precise predictions using the mathematics of logarithms to solve models of growth and decay. • I can explain the relationship between exponential and logarithmic functions.	I can use the critical mathematical modeling skills to plan, model, and predict the potential real-world situation of a disease that has reached epidemic status.
Surface-Level Success Criteria for SEL	**Deep-Level Success Criteria for SEL**	**Transfer-Level Success Criteria for SEL**
• I can represent growth or decay functions numerically and graphically. • I can identify the growth factor, initial value, and percentage of increase or decrease. • I can find precise answers to problems that require the use of the logarithm definition or properties.	• I can set up the equations of growth or decay for problems involving interest, diseases, population, and the spread of bacteria. • I can solve exponential models using logarithms. • I can write a basic exponential model and manipulate the equation into a logarithm using the definition. I can state that exponential functions and logarithms are inverses of each other.	I can synthesize my mathematics and communication skills to inform our local health department.

Stage 3: Driving Question (Written at the Transfer Level)

Driving question: Who in your hometown should address the spread of an infectious disease?

Authentic context: Students will simulate the experience of a local Center for Disease Control.

Stage 4: Tasks (Specific Strategies and Activities)

Surface-Level Content Tasks	Deep-Level Content Tasks	Transfer-Level Content Tasks
Reading: Define key terms and define mathematics models. **Mathematics or writing:** Practice skills with textbook problems. **Speaking:** In small groups, compare and contrast skills practice.	**Reading:** Read examples of how to use logarithms to solve exponential models. **Mathematics or writing:** Solve various examples of exponential growth or decay models. **Speaking:** In small classroom groups, share solutions to applications and discuss the mathematics of the problems solved.	**Reading:** Research past diseases and analyze their spread. Examples include the Spanish flu and the black plague, among other historical disease outbreaks. **Mathematics or writing:** Write models for a potential disease outbreak for your hometown. **Speaking:** Share your findings in small groups.
Surface-Level SEL Tasks	**Deep-Level SEL Tasks**	**Transfer-Level SEL Tasks**
Reading: Read and interact with the definitions of key terms for exponential and logarithmic functions. Examples include *growth rate*, *initial value*, and *half-life*. **Mathematics or writing:** Practice the skills and manipulation of exponential and logarithmic functions. **Speaking:** In small groups, work together to check your assigned skill problems and discuss your misunderstandings.	**Reading:** Read articles and watch videos on examples of exponential growth and decay. **Mathematics or writing:** Create various models and analyze those models. **Speaking:** Present your models and discuss the mathematics of your models.	**Reading:** Read the letter from the health department requesting help in planning for outbreak of a disease. **Mathematics or writing:** Analyze the spread of the disease and write a presentation that communicates the plan for a potential outbreak. **Speaking:** In a science fair–like forum, share the plan with community stakeholders.

Stage 5: Entry Event

At the start of class, show a clip from a popular zombie film to students. The video clip focuses on the rapid spread of a disease, the panic that ensues, and the need for mathematical modeling to predict characteristics of the spread. After the video, give students a letter from the health department. In the letter, students will be asked to help plan for a disease outbreak in their hometown.

Then place students into inquiry groups to generate questions they may have about preparing for such an event. Students will write their questions on sticky notes and place them on the front board. The questions will then be sorted into "mathematics," science," and other categories. Based on the mathematical inquiry, provide a minilesson to students on the basics of the unit.

Source: © 2021 by Dan Perdun. Used with permission.
Source for standards: Indiana Department of Education. (2019b). Indiana academic standards, mathematics: Algebra II. *Indianapolis, IN: Author. Accessed at www.in.gov/doe/files/Algebra-II-Math-Standards-Correlation-Guide-2020-updated.pdf on October 7, 2021.*

Example 4: Grade 8 Language Arts or Social Studies

SPBL Unit Plan

Stage 1: Learning Intentions (a Major Concept for the Unit and a CASEL Competency)

1. Content learning intention: I can apply the knowledge I have learned about lawmaking and argument writing to draft a bill and create a social justice campaign (SS 8.2.6–8.2.10; SL.4.1, SL.4.2; 8.W.3.1, 8.RV.3.2, 8.RN.2.1).

2. SEL learning intention (responsible decision making and social awareness): I can examine the process lawmakers and influencers go through to create laws and change policies. I can make responsible choices for myself and my community while looking through diverse problems and solutions.

Stage 2: Success Criteria (Daily Learning Goals)

You could have multiple goals, written without context or specificity.

Surface-Level Success Criteria for Content	Deep-Level Success Criteria for Content	Transfer-Level Success Criteria for Content
• I can define the process for making a law, including an understanding of the Bill of Rights, checks and balances, and amendments. • I can define the types of argument techniques used in writing. • I can understand propaganda and the three types of appeals.	• I can research contemporary laws in my community or state that I want changed. • I can write my own bill to change a law and create a social campaign to advocate for the change.	• I can see how the process works to create change in our country and build lasting policies that reflect the desires of the citizens. • I can appeal to all levels of readers through pathos, logos, and ethos.
Surface-Level Success Criteria for SEL	**Deep-Level Success Criteria for SEL**	**Transfer-Level Success Criteria for SEL**
• I can describe what the term *influencer* means. • I can understand *bias*, *advocate*, and *equity*.	• I can compare and contrast my personal perspective on a law and then decide how that law can have the best impact on the community. • I can understand how influencers create change.	I can apply my role as an influencer and advocate to write a bill and create an ad campaign that promotes change in a law or policy.

Stage 3: Driving Question (Written at the Transfer Level)

Driving question: To what extent can we create justice for all?

Authentic context: Students will simulate what it is like to research a law and try to make changes to the law by writing a bill and creating a social media ad campaign.

Stage 4: Tasks (Specific Strategies and Activities)

Surface-Level Content Tasks

Reading:

1. Read excerpts from the textbook on law policy.

2. Read articles on bias, influencers, and word choice or rhetoric and articles on current laws and practices in our state.

3. Read the play *Twelve Angry Men* (Rose, 2006).

Writing:

1. Engage in argument writing (creating a campaign).

2. Engage in informative writing (drafting a bill).

Speaking: Give a presentation on the campaign and mock trial.

Deep-Level Content Tasks

Reading:

1. Compare word choice and rhetoric in articles on modern law topics: gun control, immigration, and so on.

2. Examine how pathos, ethos, and logos work in a persuasive situation.

3. Compare and contrast bills that have passed and bills that have been rejected.

Writing:

1. Create a graphic organizer comparing and contrasting the word choice and examining its effectiveness with authors.

2. Draft a bill.

3. Draft an argument slogan and campaign.

Speaking:

1. Do a mock Congress, debating the bill.

2. Present the social media campaign.

Transfer-Level Content Tasks

Reading: Provide peer critiques on formal letters, offering different perspectives.

Writing:

1. Write a bill.

2. Write an argument speech to incorporate in the ad campaign.

3. Write a slogan connecting to rhetoric and persuasive techniques.

Speaking:

1. Present bills to lawyers from the community.

2. Present your ad to peers for voting.

Surface-Level SEL Tasks	Deep-Level SEL Tasks	Transfer-Level SEL Tasks
Reading: Read a short article on influencers and advocates. **Writing:** Create definitions for *personal responsibility, community,* and *influencer.* **Speaking:** Have small-group discussions about the impact of personal bias and responsibility on lawmaking.	**Reading:** Compare current influencers and their effectiveness. **Writing:** Write daily reflections on key takeaways and self-discoveries. **Speaking:** Conduct a Socratic seminar comparing and contrasting the effectiveness of different influencers' and founding fathers' persuasive and propaganda techniques.	**Reading:** Read speeches by current influencers and founding fathers. **Writing:** Compare the techniques and biases from these groups. Determine who are the better advocates. **Speaking:** Have small-group discussions and determinations on what type of rhetoric makes a person a strong influencer and advocate.

Stage 5: Entry Event
First, show a video with images reminding students of the four components of lawmaking: (1) the Bill of Rights, (2) checks and balances, (3) amendments, and (4) elections. Next, students will see a visual showcasing the twenty different rhetorical devices they have learned are used to help create change in laws. After that, students will see examples of founding fathers and bills they drafted. Up next, students will see a list of policies that are being debated right now (this list will be fluid). Then, give students a call to action. After the video, a know or need-to-know protocol, as well as a timeline and milestone checklist, will be used to start the inquiry process.

Source: © 2021 by Stephanie Barnes. Used with permission; Rose, R. (2006). Twelve angry men. *Friday Harbor, WA: Turtleback Books. (Original work written 1954)*

Source for standards: Indiana Department of Education. (2020a). Indiana academic standards, grade eight English/language arts. *Indianapolis, IN: Author. Accessed at www.in.gov/doe/files/Grade-8-ELA-Correlation-Guides-2020-updated.pdf on October 7, 2021; Indiana Department of Education. (2020c).* Indiana academic standards, social studies: Grade 8. *Indianapolis, IN: Author. Accessed at www.doe.in.gov/sites/default/files/standards/grade-8-ss-standards-2020.pdf on May 25, 2021.*

page 3 of 3

Example 5: Grade 12 Project Lead The Way—Biomedical Innovation (Problem 5: Combating a Public Health Issue)

SPBL Unit Plan
Stage 1: Learning Intentions (a Major Concept for the Unit and a CASEL Competency)
1. Content learning intention: I can apply the knowledge I gain from research on the current opioid epidemic to develop evidence-based solutions and innovative approaches to addressing this challenge (O10.2, KS10.2.1, KS10.2.2). **2. SEL learning intention (social awareness):** I can share the perspective of those impacted by addiction.
Stage 2: Success Criteria (Daily Learning Goals) *You could have multiple goals, written without context or specificity.*

Surface-Level Success Criteria for Content	Deep-Level Success Criteria for Content	Transfer-Level Success Criteria for Content

• I can list common opioids and why they are used medically.
 	
• I can define *addiction* and *tolerance* and outline how brains are altered by addiction.
 	
• I can cite key statistics that provide important context for the epidemic.
	• I can explain factors that have contributed to the three waves of the current epidemic.
	
	• I can outline multiple pathways that have led people to opioid addiction.
	
	• I can analyze potential costs and benefits of a variety of public health strategies to minimize opioid-related harms.
	
	• I can explain why garnering public support for my public health strategies could be difficult.
		• I can develop a comprehensive evidence-based strategy to:
		  – Reduce the number of new addictions
		  – Treat and rehabilitate current addicts
		  – Reduce the number of overdose deaths
		
		• I can brainstorm ways to reduce the stigma around addiction to increase public approval for funding our strategy.

Surface-Level Success Criteria for SEL	**Deep-Level Success Criteria for SEL**	**Transfer-Level Success Criteria for SEL**
I can define stigma and explain its importance in the context of treating addiction as a health concern.	I can compare and contrast a variety of attitudes and perspectives that people have about addiction.	I can empathize with individuals and families impacted by addiction.

Stage 3: Driving Question (Written at the Transfer Level)
Driving question: To what extent can we develop evidence-based strategies and new innovations to combat the current opioid epidemic? **Authentic context:** Students will simulate working on an opioid task force.

page 1 of 2

Sustainable Project-Based Learning © 2022 Solution Tree Press • SolutionTree.com
Visit **go.SolutionTree.com/21stcenturyskills** to download this free reproducible.

Stage 4: Tasks (Specific Strategies and Activities)		
Surface-Level Content Tasks **Reading:** Read articles and watch video segments introducing the epidemic. **Writing:** Create a concept map or graphic organizer of terms and statistics. **Speaking:** Do a think-pair-share of summary graphics (peer feedback protocol on graphics).	**Deep-Level Content Tasks** **Reading:** Read articles, watch video segments, and consider research focusing on how this epidemic came to be and potential solutions. **Writing:** Create a graphic organizer or timeline outlining multiple paths to addiction or death and potential points of intervention. Create graphics summarizing a variety of potential solutions or innovations. **Speaking:** Have small-group discussions and presentations of the graphics, gaining peer feedback.	**Transfer-Level Content Tasks** **Reading:** Do peer critiques of letters. **Writing:** Write a letter to a representative or other stakeholder. **Speaking:** Present an answer to the driving question to peers and community stakeholders.
Surface-Level SEL Tasks **Reading:** Read an article and watch video segments introducing stigma and empathy (chapter from *Beautiful Boy*, Sheff, 2009). **Writing:** Define what empathy is and why it matters. **Speaking:** Have small-group discussions of what empathy is and why it matters.	**Deep-Level SEL Tasks** **Reading:** Read an article on strategies to address stigma and increase empathy. **Writing:** Write an informal journal reflection about a time when you had difficulty understanding the perspective of someone else. **Speaking:** Conduct a Socratic seminar on how empathy can be developed.	**Transfer-Level SEL Tasks** **Reading:** Do peer critiques of letters. **Writing:** Incorporate empathy into your letter to a stakeholder. **Speaking:** Describe what society can do to be more aware of addiction while answering the driving question.
Stage 5: Entry Event		
Show a video collage containing headlines, images, and other compelling hooks. A know or need-to-know protocol will be used to start the inquiry process.		

Source: © 2021 by Craig Harper. Used with permission; Sheff, D. (2009). Beautiful boy: A father's journey through his son's addiction. *Boston: Mariner Books.*
Source for standards: Project Lead The Way. (2018). Biomedical innovation PLTW framework. *Accessed at https://instructional -resources.s3.amazonaws.com/PLTW_Biomedical_Science/40231_BiomedicalInnovation/English_External_Files/FWK_BI _problem5.pdf on May 25, 2021.*

Example 6: Grades 11–12 Data Analytics

SPBL Unit Plan
Stage 1: Learning Intentions (a Major Concept for the Unit and a CASEL Competency)
1. Content learning intention: I can use my understanding of data to transform and communicate data as critical to responsible decision making (3B-AP-15, 3A-AP-16, 3A-AP-18). **2. SEL learning intention (responsible decision making):** I can utilize principles of data analytics to gather, analyze, and make decisions based on ethically sourced data.
Stage 2: Success Criteria (Daily Learning Goals) *You could have multiple goals, written without context or specificity.*

Surface-Level Success Criteria for Content	Deep-Level Success Criteria for Content	Transfer-Level Success Criteria for Content
I can restate analytic models or describe visualizations for a given data set.	I can analyze data using R code to clean data sets, create analytic models, and create visualizations.	I can compile a data set from primary sources or an original collection and then utilize R code to clean data sets, create analytic models, and create visualizations for a given data set.
Surface-Level Success Criteria for SEL	**Deep-Level Success Criteria for SEL**	**Transfer-Level Success Criteria for SEL**
I can describe what *ethically sourced data* means.	I can use data sets to compare and contrast different perspectives on a community issue.	I can present data that I have collected and analyzed related to a community issue to support my perspective and outline a solution.

Stage 3: Driving Question (Written at the Transfer Level)
Driving question: When is it appropriate and ethical to use information gleaned from past observations in order to make informed decisions and predictions about the future? **Authentic context:** Students will collect, clean, and analyze data and create a visualization answering a measurable question of meaning to the local community.

Stage 4: Tasks (Specific Strategies and Activities)

Surface-Level Content Tasks

Reading: Read a short article on how to conduct a design review protocol.

Writing: Define key terms to develop a course glossary.

Speaking: Present conclusions from a design review protocol.

Deep-Level Content Tasks

Reading: Compare the data-cleaning process in R versus in Python.

Writing: Create a diagram comparing and contrasting data mining and big data.

Speaking: Conduct a Harkness seminar on data visualization about home ownership by neighborhood.

Transfer-Level Content Tasks

Reading: Do a peer review of data analysis and visualizations created by classmates.

Writing: Create a program in the R programming language to clean a data set.

Speaking: Present answers to the driving question or a student-created data visualization.

Surface-Level SEL Tasks

Reading: Read an article about ethically sourced data.

Writing: Define key data-sourcing terms such as *AIDC, fuzzy logic,* and *recommendation engine.*

Speaking: Have small-group discussions on what *ethical data* means.

Deep-Level SEL Tasks

Reading: Read an article comparing decision-making models.

Writing: Write a journal article reflecting on the data collection attempts blocked over twenty-four hours when using the DuckDuckGo web browser.

Speaking: Conduct a Socratic seminar comparing and contrasting the roles of data in the following decision-making styles: analytical, behavioral, conceptual, and directive.

Transfer-Level SEL Tasks

Reading: Read an article about the future changes in data collection implied by Apple's App Tracking Transparency policy.

Writing: Write an action plan for a community issue you have studied.

Speaking: Describe a case study of unethically sourced data and the limits people and organizations face when they commit to ethically sourced data.

Stage 5: Entry Event

Students will develop questions about data analytics as a career field in advance of a panel with data analysts from Northwestern Mutual. Three students in the class will attend a training to facilitate the panel and work as facilitators or hosts for the event.

Source: © 2021 by Christopher Kjaer. Used with permission.
Source for standards: Computer Science Teachers Association. (2017). K–12 computer science standards, revised 2017. Accessed at www.doe.k12.de.us/cms/lib/DE01922744/Centricity/Domain/176/CSTA%20Computer%20Science%20Standards%20 Revised%202017.pdf on May 25, 2021.

Example 7: Grades 11–12 English (AP Literature)

SPBL Unit Plan

Stage 1: Learning Intentions (a Major Concept for the Unit and a CASEL Competency)

1. Content learning intention: I can apply my understanding of satirical techniques to create a satire that communicates a message of change (RL.11-12.1, RL.11-12.2, RL.11-12.4, RL.11-12.6, W.11-12.1, W.11-12.4, W.11-12.7, SL.11-12.1, SL.11-12.4, L.11-12.3).

2. SEL learning intention (social awareness): I can understand multiple perspectives of cultural and social issues.

Stage 2: Success Criteria (Daily Learning Goals)

You could have multiple goals, written without context or specificity.

Surface-Level Success Criteria for Content	Deep-Level Success Criteria for Content	Transfer-Level Success Criteria for Content
• I can identify key literary techniques such as irony, sarcasm, incongruity, hyperbole, and so on. • I can define tone words used to describe satire, such as *facetious, sardonic, droll,* and so on.	I can analyze how literary techniques are used to create humor and social commentary.	I can apply my understanding of satirical techniques to create a satire that communicates a message of change.
Surface-Level Success Criteria for SEL	**Deep-Level Success Criteria for SEL**	**Transfer-Level Success Criteria for SEL**
I can identify the social issues writers want to address.	I can objectively analyze several perspectives involved in social issues.	I can empathize with those who have different perspectives.

Stage 3: Driving Question (Written at the Transfer Level)

Driving question: To what extent is satire effective in developing social commentary to communicate a message of change?

Authentic context: Students will use literary tools to create a satire that communicates a message of change as a way to understand how writers of all mediums effectively develop social commentary (journalists, theater directors, media content writers, comedians, and so on).

Stage 4: Tasks (Specific Strategies and Activities)

Surface-Level Content Tasks	Deep-Level Content Tasks	Transfer-Level Content Tasks
Reading: Choose a satirical play to read with a literature circle, such as *The Importance of Being Earnest* (Wilde, 1980), *Pygmalion* (Shaw, 1912), or *The Taming of the Shrew* (Shakespeare, 1998). **Writing:** Define and identify text examples of literary techniques. **Speaking:** Engage in literature circle discussions to identify literary techniques and tones.	**Reading:** Analyze how the literary techniques in the satirical play create humor and social commentary using a text-evidence graphic organizer. **Writing:** Compose analytical argument essays for question two (prose analysis) and question three (theme analysis) of sample AP literature writing prompts. **Speaking:** Engage in literature circle discussions to compare the play to modern satires that provide social commentary.	**Reading:** Research the social issue for the satire you will compose, using a graphic organizer to record varying perspectives on the issue. **Writing:** Compose a modern satire on a social issue in any choice of form—script, visual, speech, and so on. **Speaking:** Present satires to a target audience.
Surface-Level SEL Tasks	**Deep-Level SEL Tasks**	**Transfer-Level SEL Tasks**
Reading: Explore supplemental examples of satire during minilessons to practice identifying perspectives. **Writing:** Make a list of social issues the writer addresses in the play and what perspectives are presented and missing. **Speaking:** Share examples of perspectives in literature circle discussions.	**Reading:** Compare the satirical play to a modern satire on the same issue to analyze several perspectives. **Writing:** Draw conclusions and write about how and why the perspectives have changed or shifted. **Speaking:** Engage in the Six Thinking Hats process (de Bono, 1999) to discuss and analyze different perspectives in satires.	**Reading:** Review peers' satires to provide feedback on how they include an array of perspectives. **Writing:** Focus on adding humor techniques to the satire that will help the audience appreciate and empathize with diverse perspectives. **Speaking:** Present the satire in a way that is respectful of all perspectives and persuades the audience of a social change.

Stage 5: Entry Event

Students will view several video clips, editorial comics, and fiction or nonfiction texts to begin pondering whether the pieces are satire or comedy, satire or derision, and satire or truth. After viewing each example, students will record their lingering questions. Once the driving question is introduced, students will begin to brainstorm questions for what they need to know in regard to the definitions, purposes, and boundaries of satire.

Source: © 2021 by Cristen Cassler. Used with permission; Shakespeare, W. (1998). The taming of the shrew. New York: Signet Classic. (Original work published 1594); Shaw, G. B. (1912). Pygmalion. Accessed at https://www.gutenberg.org/files/3825 /3825-h/3825-h.htm on February 7, 2022; Wilde, O. (1980). The importance of being earnest. New York: Samuel French. (Original work published 1895)
Source for standards: National Governors Association Center for Best Practices & Council of Chief State School Officers. (2010). Common Core State Standards for English language arts and literacy in history/social studies, science, and technical subjects. Washington, DC: Authors. Accessed at www.corestandards.org/assets/CCSSI_ELA%20Standards.pdf on October 7, 2021.

REFERENCES AND RESOURCES

American Foundation for Suicide Prevention. (n.d.). *Suicide statistics.* Accessed at https://afsp.org /suicide-statistics on May 24, 2021.

Antislavery.org. (2021). *What is modern slavery?* Accessed at www.antislavery.org/slavery-today/modern-slavery on December 8, 2021.

Armstrong, C., Oliver, J., Seacrest, R., Ackerman, R., & Sher, A. (Executive producers). (2010–2011). *Jamie Oliver's food revolution* [TV series]. Los Angeles: Ryan Seacrest Productions.

Banchi, H., & Bell, R. (2008). The many levels of inquiry. *Science and Children, 46*(2), 26–29.

Baron, D. (2017). *Examining student work: A constructivist protocol.* Accessed at www.nsrfharmony.org /wp-content/uploads/2017/10/constructivist_student.pdf on December 10, 2021.

Battelle for Kids. (2021). *Partnership for 21st century learning.* Accessed at www.battelleforkids.org/networks/p21 on November 5, 2021.

Bayewitz, M. D., Cunningham, S. A., Ianora, J. A., Jones, B., Nielsen, M., Remmert, W., et al. (2020). *Help your team: Overcoming common collaborative challenges in a PLC at Work.* Bloomington, IN: Solution Tree Press.

Birkett, T. (1997). *Truax.* Memphis, TN: National Oak Flooring Manufacturers Association.

Bloom, H. (1988). *George Bernard Shaw's Pygmalion.* New York: Chelsea House Publishers.

Bloomberg, P., & Pitchford, B. (2017). *Leading impact teams: Building a culture of efficacy.* Thousand Oaks, CA: Corwin.

Boss, S. (2018). *Project based teaching: How to create rigorous and engaging learning experiences.* Alexandria, VA: Association for Supervision and Curriculum Development.

Carmel High School. (2018). *Senior survey.* Carmel, IN: Author.

Climate Reality. (2018, December 4). *24 hours of reality: "Earthrise" by Amanda Gorman* [Video]. Accessed at www.youtube.com/watch?v=xwOvBv8RLmo on October 8, 2021.

Collaborative for Academic, Social, and Emotional Learning (CASEL). (n.d.a). *Our history.* Accessed at https://casel.org/about-us/our-history on December 8, 2021.

Collaborative for Academic, Social, and Emotional Learning (CASEL). (n.d.b). *What is the CASEL framework?* Accessed at https://casel.org/fundamentals-of-sel/what-is-the-casel-framework on December 8, 2021.

Computer Science Teachers Association. (2017). *K–12 computer science standards, revised 2017.* Accessed at www.doe.k12.de.us/cms/lib/DE01922744/Centricity/Domain/176/CSTA%20Computer%20Science%20 Standards%20Revised%202017.pdf on May 25, 2021.

Conzemius, A. E., & O'Neill, J. (2014). *The handbook for SMART school teams: Revitalizing best practices for collaboration* (2nd ed.). Bloomington, IN: Solution Tree Press.

Cornell University. (n.d.a). *Qualitative assessment tools.* Accessed at https://scl.cornell.edu/staff/assessment-and -planning/methodology-tools/qualitative-assessment-tools on May 21, 2021.

Cornell University. (n.d.b). *Quantitative assessment tools.* Accessed at https://scl.cornell.edu/staff/assessment-and -planning/methodology-tools/quantitative-assessment-tools on May 21, 2021.

Courchesne, C. G. (2005, Spring). "A suggestion of a fundamental nature": Imagining a legal education of solely electives taught as discussions. *Rutgers Law Record, 29*(21), 21–63.

Davis, J. (2021). *Goal setting protocol.* Accessed at www.schoolreforminitiative.org/download/goal-setting -protocol on January 23, 2022.

de Bono, E. (1999). *Six thinking hats* (Revised and updated ed.). Boston: Back Bay Books.

Dewey, J. (1933). *How we think: A restatement of the relation of reflective thinking to the educative process.* Boston: D. C. Heath.

Dintersmith, T. (Producer), & Whiteley, G. (Director). (2018). *Most likely to succeed* [Motion picture]. Boston: EDU21C Foundation.

Doig, B., & Groves, S. (2011). Japanese lesson study: Teacher professional development through communities of inquiry. *Mathematics Teacher Education and Development, 13*(1), 77–93.

Doran, G. T. (1981). There's a S.M.A.R.T. way to write management's goals and objectives. *Management Review, 70*(11), 35–36.

Dr. Seuss. (1971). *The Lorax.* New York: Random House.

DuFour, R. (2004). What is a professional learning community? *Educational Leadership, 61*(8), 6–11.

DuFour, R. (2015). *In praise of American educators: And how they can become even better.* Bloomington, IN: Solution Tree Press.

DuFour, R., DuFour, R., Eaker, R., & Many, T. W. (2010). *Learning by doing: A handbook for Professional Learning Communities at Work* (2nd ed.). Bloomington, IN: Solution Tree Press.

DuFour, R., DuFour, R., Eaker, R., Many, T. W., & Mattos, M. (2016). *Learning by doing: A handbook for Professional Learning Communities at Work* (3rd ed.). Bloomington, IN: Solution Tree Press.

EL Education. (2017). Fishbowl protocol. In *EL Education: Classroom protocols* (p. 17). Accessed at https:// curriculum.eleducation.org/sites/default/files/curriculumtools_classroomprotocols_053017.pdf on February 14, 2022.

The Enneagram Institute®. (2021). *The nine enneagram type descriptions.* Accessed at www.enneagraminstitute .com/type-descriptions on December 8, 2021.

Finneran, P. (2014). *Documentary impact: Social change through storytelling.* Toronto, Ontario, Canada: Inspirit Foundation.

Free the Slaves. (2021). *Our work: Global strategic plan.* Accessed at www.freetheslaves.net/our-model-for -freedom/strategic-plan on December 8, 2021.

Hammond, Z. (2015a). *Culturally responsive teaching and the brain: Promoting authentic engagement and rigor among culturally and linguistically diverse students.* Thousand Oaks, CA: Corwin.

Hammond, Z, (2015b). *Four tools for interrupting implicit bias.* Accessed at https://crtandthebrain.com /four-tools-for-interrupting-implicit-bias on November 12, 2021.

Hammond, Z. (2020). The power of protocols for equity. *Educational Leadership, 77*(7), 45–50.

Hattie, J. A. C. (2009). *Visible learning: A synthesis of over 800 meta-analyses relating to achievement.* London: Routledge.

Indiana Department of Education. (2016). *Biology science standards.* Indianapolis, IN: Author. Accessed at www.in.gov/doe/files/indiana-biology-standards-2016-41116.pdf on October 7, 2021.

Indiana Department of Education. (2019a). *Indiana academic standards, mathematics: Algebra I*. Indianapolis, IN: Author. Accessed at www.doe.in.gov/sites/default/files/standards/algebra-i-standards-dec-2020.pdf on October 7, 2021.

Indiana Department of Education. (2019b). *Indiana academic standards, mathematics: Algebra II*. Indianapolis, IN: Author. Accessed at www.in.gov/doc/files/Algebra-II-Math-Standards-Correlation-Guide-2020-updated .pdf on October 7, 2021.

Indiana Department of Education. (2020a). *Indiana academic standards, grade eight English/language arts*. Indianapolis, IN: Author. Accessed at www.in.gov/doe/files/Grade-8-ELA-Correlation-Guides-2020-updated .pdf on October 7, 2021.

Indiana Department of Education. (2020b). *Indiana academic standards, mathematics: Grade 8*. Indianapolis, IN: Author. Accessed at www.doe.in.gov/sites/default/files/standards/grade8-math-standards-dec-2020.pdf on October 7, 2021.

Indiana Department of Education. (2020c). *Indiana academic standards, social studies: Grade 8*. Indianapolis, IN: Author. Accessed at www.doe.in.gov/sites/default/files/standards/grade-8-ss-standards-2020.pdf on May 25, 2021.

Jagers, R. J., Randall-Garner, P., & Van Ausdal, K. (2018, February 5). *Leveraging SEL to promote equity: What educators need to know and do*. Accessed at https://casel.org/wp-content/uploads/2018/02/equity-webinar -FINAL.pdf on May 21, 2021.

Jagers, R. J., Rivas-Drake, D., & Williams, B. (2019). Transformative social and emotional learning (SEL): Toward SEL in service of educational equity and excellence. *Educational Psychologist, 54*(3), 162–184.

Jones, S. M., & Kahn, J. (2017). *The evidence base for how we learn: Supporting students' social, emotional, and academic development*. Washington, DC: Aspen Institute. Accessed at https://files.eric.ed.gov/fulltext /ED577039.pdf on May 21, 2021.

Kamps, K. (2021, January 27). *Promoting a PBL mindset: The "dimmer switch" approach*. Accessed at www.pblworks.org/blog/promoting-pbl-mindset-dimmer-switch-approach on May 24, 2021.

Krajcik, J., Schneider, B., Miller, E., Chen, I.-C., Bradford, L., Bartz, K., et al. (2021). *Assessing the effect of ML-PBL on science learning*. Accessed at https://mlpbl.open3d.science/techreport on May 24, 2021.

Larmer, J. (2012). *What does it take for a project to be fully "authentic"?* Accessed at www.edutopia.org/blog /authentic-project-based-learning-john-larmer on November 5, 2021.

Larmer, J., & Mergendoller, J. R. (2010). Seven essentials for project-based learning. *Educational Leadership, 68*(1), 34–37. Accessed at www.ascd.org/publications/educational_leadership/sept10/vol68/num01 /Seven_Essentials_for_Project-Based_Learning.aspx on May 21, 2011.

Lencioni, P. (2005). *Overcoming the five dysfunctions of a team: A field guide for leaders, managers, and facilitators*. San Francisco: Jossey-Bass.

Lincoln, A. (1863). "The Gettysburg Address." *The National Archives*. Accessed at www.archives.gov/historical -docs/todays-doc/?dod-date=1119 on October 30, 2021.

Lucas Education Research. (2021). *Project-based learning increases science achievement in elementary school and advances social and emotional learning*. Accessed at www.lucasedresearch.org/wp-content/uploads/2021/01 /MLPBL-Research-Brief-1.pdf on May 24, 2021.

Marzano, R. J. (2004). *Building background knowledge for academic achievement: Research on what works in schools*. Alexandria, VA: Association for Supervision and Curriculum Development.

Marzano, R. J. (2017). *The new art and science of teaching*. Bloomington, IN: Solution Tree Press.

Marzano, R. J., Parsley, D., Gagnon, D., & Norford, J. (2020). *Teacher as researcher*. Marzano Research. Accessed at www.marzanoresearch.com/wp-content/uploads/2021/06/Teacher-as-Researcher-White-Paper-1 .pdf on December 2, 2021.

Massachusetts Department of Elementary and Secondary Education. (2014). *Massachusetts Vocational Technical Education Framework: Agriculture and natural resources occupational cluster—Environmental science and technology.* Accessed at www.doe.mass.edu/ccte/cvte/frameworks/enviroscitech.pdf on October 8, 2021.

Maxwell, M., Stobaugh, R., & Tassell, J. L. (2016). *Real-world learning framework for secondary schools: Digital tools and practical strategies for successful implementation.* Bloomington, IN: Solution Tree Press.

McDowell, M. (2017). *Rigorous PBL by design: Three shifts for developing confident and competent learners.* Thousand Oaks, CA: Corwin.

McDowell, M. (2021). *Teaching for transfer: A guide for designing learning with real-world application.* Bloomington, IN: Solution Tree Press.

National Commission on Social, Emotional, and Academic Development. (2017). *How learning happens: Supporting students' social, emotional, and academic development.* Washington, DC: Aspen Institute. Accessed at www.aspeninstitute.org/wp-content/uploads/2018/01/2017_Aspen_InterimReport_Update2.pdf on October 5, 2021.

National Commission on Social, Emotional, and Academic Development. (2018). *From a nation at risk to a nation at hope: Recommendations from the National Commission on Social, Emotional, and Academic Development.* Washington, DC: Aspen Institute. Accessed at http://nationathope.org/wp-content/uploads/2018_aspen_final-report_full_webversion.pdf on October 5, 2021.

National Council for the Social Studies. *College, career, and civic life (C3) framework for social studies state standards: Guidance for enhancing the rigor of K–12 civics, economics, geography, and history.* Accessed at www.socialstudies.org/standards/c3 on January 3, 2022.

National Governors Association Center for Best Practices & Council of Chief State School Officers. (2010). *Common Core State Standards for English language arts and literacy in history/social studies, science, and technical subjects.* Washington, DC: Authors. Accessed at www.corestandards.org/assets/CCSSI_ELA%20Standards.pdf on October 7, 2021.

National Institute of Mental Health. (2021). *Mental illness.* Accessed at www.nimh.nih.gov/health/statistics/mental-illness on May 24, 2021.

New Tech Network. (n.d.). *What we do.* Accessed at https://newtechnetwork.org/what-we-do on February 26, 2020.

NGSS Lead States. (2013). *Next Generation Science Standards: For states, by states.* Washington, DC: The National Academies Press.

Parsons, R. D., & Brown, K. S. (2002). *Teacher as reflective practitioner and action researcher.* Belmont, CA: Wadsworth.

PBLWorks. (n.d.). *What is PBL?* Accessed at www.pblworks.org/what-is-pbl on May 21, 2021.

PBLWorks. (2019). *Essential project design elements checklist.* Accessed at https://my.pblworks.org/resource/document/pbl_essential_elements_checklist?fbclid=IwAR3cGqU1Y6WEXSgVnrto2WQZ0weKKQl_kLJr_DNDkZuDdgj_wjyBYbv249c on May 21, 2021.

PBLWorks. (2021). *Gold standard PBL: Essential project design elements.* Accessed at www.pblworks.org/what-is-pbl/gold-standard-project-design on November 13, 2021.

Project Lead The Way. (2018). *Biomedical innovation PLTW framework.* Accessed at https://instructional-resources.s3.amazonaws.com/PLTW_Biomedical_Science/40231_BiomedicalInnovation/English_External_Files/FWK_BI_problem5.pdf on May 25, 2021.

Rose, R. (2006). *Twelve angry men.* Friday Harbor, WA: Turtleback Books. (Original work written 1954)

Saavedra, A. R., Liu, Y., Haderlein, S. K., Rapaport, A., Garland, M., Hoepfner, D., et al. (2021, February 22). *Knowledge in action efficacy study over two years.* Los Angeles: Dornsife Center for Economic and Social Research, University of Southern California. Accessed at https://cesr.usc.edu/sites/default/files/Knowledge%20in%20Action%20Efficacy%20Study_18feb2021_final.pdf on May 24, 2021.

Schlechty, P. C. (2001). *Shaking up the schoolhouse: How to support and sustain educational innovation.* San Francisco: Jossey-Bass.

School Reform Initiative. (2017a). *The Charrette protocol.* Accessed at www.schoolreforminitiative.org/download /charrette-protocol on January 27, 2022.

School Reform Initiative. (2017b.). *Peer coaching: Observer as coach.* Accessed at www.schoolreforminitiative.org /download/peer-coaching-observer-as-coach on January 23, 2022.

School Reform Initiative. (2017c). *Tuning protocol guidelines.* Accessed at www.schoolreforminitiative.org /download/tuning-protocol-guidelines on January 27, 2022.

Shakespeare, W. (1998). *The taming of the shrew.* New York: Signet Classic. (Original work published 1594)

Shaw, G. B. (1912). *Pygmalion.* Accessed at https://www.gutenberg.org/files/3825/3825-h/3825-h.htm on February 7, 2022.

Sheff, D. (2009). *Beautiful boy: A father's journey through his son's addiction.* Boston: Mariner Books.

Sierra Club. (2021). *Earthrise poem by Amanda Gorman.* Accessed at www.sierraclub.org/los-padres /blog/2021/02/earthrise-poem-amanda-gorman on January 10, 2022.

Singleton, G. E., & Linton, C. (2022). *Courageous conversations about race: A field guide for achieving equity in schools.* Thousand Oaks, CA: Corwin.

Skinner, B. F. (1964). New methods and new aims in teaching. *New Scientist, 122.* Accessed at file:///C:/Users /brad.sever/Downloads/New-Methods-aims-in-Teach%20(1).pdf on November 1, 2021.

Spurlock, M. (Director). (2004). *Super size me* [Film]. Los Angeles: The Con.

Steinberg, A. (1998). *Real learning, real work: School-to-work as high school reform.* New York: Routledge.

Stowe, H. B. (1853). *Uncle Tom's cabin; or, life among the lowly.* Boston: J. P. Jewett.

Terada, Y. (2021, February 21). *New research makes a powerful case for PBL.* Accessed at www.edutopia.org /article/new-research-makes-powerful-case-pbl on May 24, 2021.

Thompson-Grove, G. (2017). *What? So what? Now what?* Accessed at www.schoolreforminitiative.org/download /what-so-what-now-what on December 10, 2021.

Vernon, D. T., & Blake, R. L. (1993). Does problem-based learning work? A meta-analysis of evaluative research. *Academic Medicine, 68*(7), 550–563.

Visible Learning+. (n.d.). *The visible learning research.* Accessed at www.visiblelearning.com/content /visible-learning-research on May 21, 2021.

Visible Learning Meta[X]. (n.d.). *Global research database.* Accessed at www.visiblelearningmetax.com/Influences on May 21, 2021.

Visible Learning Meta[X]. (2021). *Meta[X] influence glossary.* Accessed at www.visiblelearningmetax.com/content /influence_glossary.pdf on May 21, 2021.

Waack, S. (2018, March 7). *Collective teacher efficacy (CTE) according to John Hattie.* Accessed at http://visible-learning.org/2018/03/collective-teacher-efficacy-hattie on May 21, 2021.

Weintraub, J. (Producer), & Avildsen, J. (Director). (1984). *The karate kid* [Motion picture]. Culver City, CA: Columbia Pictures.

WIDA. (2020). *WIDA English language development standards framework, 2020 edition: Kindergarten–grade 12.* Accessed at https://wida.wisc.edu/sites/default/files/resource/WIDA-ELD-Standards-Framework-2020 -Edition-Grades-9-12.pdf on October 7, 2021.

Wilde, O. (1980). *The importance of being earnest.* New York: Samuel French. (Original work published 1895)

Wiliam, D. (2017). *Embedded formative assessment* (2nd ed.). Bloomington, IN: Solution Tree Press.

INDEX

Implementing Project-Based Learning
Suzie Boss
Explore how project-based learning (PBL) has the potential to fully engage students of the digital age. Discover user-friendly strategies for implementing PBL to equip students with essential 21st century skills, strengthen their problem-solving abilities, and prepare them for college and careers.
BKF681

Bringing Innovation to School
Suzie Boss
Activate your students' creativity and problem-solving potential with breakthrough learning projects. Across all grades and content areas, student-driven collaborative projects will teach students how to generate innovative ideas and then put them into action.
BKF546

Real-World Learning Framework for Secondary Schools
Marge Maxwell, Rebecca Stobaugh, and Janet Lynne Tassell
Using the Create Excellence Framework, educators can help students find greater fulfillment in learning, while also meeting the guidelines of curriculum standards. Explore the framework's main components, and understand how to use the framework for classroom, school, and district pursuits.
BKF656

Teaching for Transfer
Michael McDowell
Empower students to become creative, well-rounded citizens, prepared to meet and overcome real-world challenges. With *Teaching for Transfer*, you will discover a road map for reconfiguring K–12 classroom instruction to ensure learners can expertly apply their knowledge and skills to new contexts.
BKF950

Problems-First Learning
Ted McCain
Discover a compelling alternative to traditional teaching practices: the problems-first instructional method. Using this method, you will fully engage students by first introducing a problem and then empowering learners to solve it using creativity, collaboration, and other essential skills.
BKF944

Solution Tree | Press   *a division of*   Solution Tree   Visit SolutionTree.com or call 800.733.6786 to order.

Wait! Your professional development journey doesn't have to end with the last pages of this book.

We realize improving student learning doesn't happen overnight. And your school or district shouldn't be left to puzzle out all the details of this process alone.

No matter where you are on the journey, we're committed to helping you get to the next stage.

Take advantage of everything from **custom workshops** to **keynote presentations** and **interactive web and video conferencing**. We can even help you develop an action plan tailored to fit your specific needs.

Let's get the conversation started.

Call 888.763.9045 today.

 SolutionTree.com